Progress in IS

More information about this series at http://www.springer.com/series/10440

Jan Huntgeburth

Developing and Evaluating a Cloud Service Relationship Theory

This book is based on a doctoral thesis successfully defended at the Business School of the University of Mannheim

 Springer

Jan Huntgeburth
Faculty of Business and Economics
Universität Augsburg
Augsburg
Germany

ISSN 2196-8705   ISSN 2196-8713   (electronic)
ISBN 978-3-319-10279-5   ISBN 978-3-319-10280-1   (eBook)
DOI 10.1007/978-3-319-10280-1

Library of Congress Control Number: 2014948062

Springer Cham Heidelberg New York Dordrecht London

Printed on acid-free paper

Springer is part of Springer Science+Business Media (www.springer.com)

Foreword

Cloud computing is an innovative technology which is now fundamentally transforming many industries. The fact that cloud computing is transforming IT product markets into IT service markets potentially inflates the highest impact in this sector since many years. More and more companies do no longer employ innovative software products "on premise"—i.e., using their own hardware infrastructure—but "off premise"—i.e., as an on-demand service, which is hosted on infrastructures owned and operated by the vendors. This leads to major transformations within both the software industry as well as nearly all other industries as they are highly dependent on digital and digitally mediated infrastructures. The megatrend within this development is that the value performance of these digital infrastructures is moved from the demand side to the supply side and is no longer operated by the demand side companies or individuals themselves. This leads to a large number of different effects in business processes and business models of the involved firms. Also, a number of insourcing and outsourcing decisions have to be revised in the light of these developments. In many cases, this leads to a revision of firm's strategies and tactics regarding their acting within global markets.

The relevant dimensions along which these decisions are taken, are on the one hand the costs, the efficiency, and the effectiveness of these solutions. On the other hand, more and more additional factors like the service level, confidentiality and privacy, as well as digital sovereignty of client actors play a major role. Especially in globally acting IT service companies, it is completely nontransparent for users and the demand side companies of such digital services, where exactly data are stored, processed, and hosted. These reasons lead to a number of relevant influence factors, which determine the propensity of clients to adopt and continue to use cloud-based digital infrastructures and services. In his work, Dr. Huntgeburth is investigating these factors and carves out the complex factors and decision processes, which are underlying contemporary decisions in cloud-based IT infrastructure situations in contrast to classically product centric IT markets. He focuses mainly on the relationship into which a client enters when beginning an interaction with a cloud provider and sheds light on the decision factors as well as the determinants of a continued usage of such services. Furthermore, he highlights the research demand for further investigating the factors of acceptance and skepticism of clients in cloud-sourcing contracts. He elaborates on the causalities, theoretical implications, and the practical contributions of this work. From the findings, Dr. Huntgeburth provides in this book, recommendations for political decision makers, managers and IT service providers can be derived.

Dr. Huntgeburth delivers a comprehensive study contributing to the body of knowledge in business research using theories and approaches from the Information Systems and the Innovation Management fields. He takes a positivist stance and grounds his viewpoint on classical economic theories like the principal agent theory.

This book delivers both a contribution to the state-of-the-art in business information systems research as well as a contribution to practitioners, who struggle to deal with the complexity of cloud computing solutions in everyday business decisions of their companies.

I would like to wish all possible success to this book, particularly its author and insightful pleasure to its many readers.

Augsburg and Prien am Chiemsee, July 2014   Daniel Veit

Preface

"The Ph.D. is about you."

At a Ph.D. colloquium, a senior scholar of my research discipline taught us once the lesson that the outcome of a Ph.D. should be far more than the final thesis or another fancy academic title. Rather, doing a Ph.D. should be about self-improvement and about being better than you were the day before. Having completed my Ph.D. at the University of Mannheim, I am fortunate to say that I have spent most of my personal resources during the last 4 years on developing myself, my way of thinking, my way of working, and my way of interacting with people. Achievements and failures were equally important experiences on the way to completing it. The content of this book presents my reflections and best research practices of 4 years of studying socio-technical phenomena surrounding cloud computing. There are many people who I like to thank for encouraging, supporting, and inspiring me over the last 4 years in this process.

I am especially grateful with my supervisor, Prof. Dr. Daniel Veit with whom I enjoyed a very productive and collaborative relationship over the last few years. It was Daniel who gained me access to so many valuable resources. Between 2010 and 2014, I was honored to discuss my cloud research at various national (MKWI 2012, Braunschweig, Germany; WI 2013, Leipzig, Germany, MKWI 2014, Paderborn, Germany) and international conferences (ECIS 2013, Utrecht, Netherlands; ICIS 2013, Milano, Italy; ECIS 2014, Tel Aviv, Israel), workshops (ICIS 2012, Orlando, USA) as well as research seminars (University of Mannheim 2010–2013, Copenhagen Business School 2011–2014, University of Augsburg 2013–2014). I also contributed as a coauthor to one journal article on cloud computing (Hauff, S.; Huntgeburth, J.; Veit, D. (2014) Exploring Uncertainties in a Marketplace for Cloud Computing: A Revelatory Case Study, *Journal of Business Economics*, February 2014). Without Daniel's encouragement and his academic leadership, this cloud publication record could not have been achieved.

Moreover, Daniel enabled me to spend 2 months at US research University. In April 2012, I was a McBride Fellow at Baylor University, Waco, Texas invited by Prof. Dorothy Leidner. During the time, Dorothy provided me with insights on Baylor's Ph.D. program. I had the chance to participate in courses and in a Ph.D.

retreat and experienced a collaborative relationship with my fellow Ph.D. students among others Pat Curry and Puzant Balozian. Just 1 year later in March/April 2013, I visited Washington State University (WSU) as a Visiting Scholar invited by Prof. Suprateek Sarker. I again participated in courses and discussed with Supra and his wife Prof. Saonee Sarker my research projects. I admire both for their passion in conducting IS research and I am very thankful for their hospitality during my stay in Pullman. Although my time at WSU was short, I have to thank Chris Calif, Xiao Xiao, Tanya Beaulieu and Lael Gatewood for making me quickly feel part of their team. Overall, the research stays abroad have enabled me to build an international network of research fellows with who I like to continue collaborating in the future.

However, my strongest sources of influence have always been my colleagues at the chair. I have learned many things from Manuel Trenz and Dennis Steininger about research, about working and about life. During our almost 3 years as research and teaching assistant at University of Mannheim, Manuel, Dennis and I have intensively supported Daniel in transforming his chair. When we left Mannheim in February 2013, the chair was characterized by many motivated students, efficient administrative processes and an excellent publication output. Both Dennis' and Manual's passion and persistence were an inspiration for me to delivering high quality results. I also like to thank my former colleagues Dr. Nils Parasie, Dr. Martin Barth, Dr. Sabine Stollhof, Dr. Georg Buss, Dr. Eva Peslova, Dr. Philipp Wunderlich, Sabine Koch, Jens Förderer, Amelie Sach, Sabrina Hauff, An Bui, and Seda Yagci for great discussions and for creating an atmosphere where I enjoyed coming to work every day.

Let me finally address some personal words to my family and friends. Thank you for supporting me in what I do and giving me confidence in being able to overcome any difficulties on my way. Without you I would have never pursued a Ph.D. and would not be the person I am today.

Munich, July 2014   Jan Huntgeburth

Contents

Abbreviations

ASP	Application service provisioning
ATT	Attentiveness to alternatives
AVA	Perceived availability concerns
AVE	Average variance extracted
CMV	Common method variance
CONT	Continuance Intention
DIA	Perceived service diagnosticity
IMC	Instructional manipulation check
IS	Information system
IT	Information technology
KNOW	Knowledge about cloud
LS	Perceived legal sanctions
NWOM	Perceived negative WOM influence
PAD	Perceived peer adoption
PLS	Partial least square
PLS-MGA	PLS multigroup analysis
PRIV	Perceived privacy concerns
PWOM	Perceived positive WOM influence
SEC	Perceived security concerns
SEM	Structural equation modelling
SLA	Service level agreement
TPA	Perceived third-party assurance
VIF	Variance inflation factor
WOM	Word-of-mouth

Chapter 1
Introduction

The computer industry is the only industry that is more fashion-driven than women's fashion. Maybe I'm an idiot, but I have no idea what anyone is talking about. What is it? It's complete gibberish. It's insane. When is this idiocy going to stop? [...] But I don't understand what we would do differently in the light of cloud computing other than change the wording of some of our ads.
Larry Ellison (2008) at the Oracle OpenWorld Congress, San Francisco

Abstract This introductory chapter outlines in four parts how this dissertation develops and evaluates a cloud service relationship theory. First, the multifaceted cloud movement shaking information technology (IT) providers, IT departments and IT users and thus, the IT industry as a whole is explained. Second, the information systems (IS) research discipline to whose knowledge base this dissertation aims to contribute is introduced. Third, the research questions and expected theoretical and practical contributions of the dissertation are outlined. Finally, a brief outlook on the remaining chapters is given.

1.1 Practical Motivation

Cloud computing is a multifaceted movement that is supposed to redefine how markets offer (Bain and Company 2012), IT departments manage (Deloitte 2009) and users consume IT (Accenture 2011; Armbrust et al. 2010; Harris et al. 2012). From a technical point of view, cloud computing is a style of computing where IT resources are offered in different granularities as-a-service over the internet (Huntgeburth et al. 2012). The idea of cloud computing has its roots in the 1960s, when the vision of "utility computing" was an essential driver of the internet evolution (Venters and Whitley 2012). A number of technological and societal advances such as the wide availability of broadband internet, increased processing power of computers, and the increasing standardization of hardware and software

© Springer International Publishing Switzerland 2015
J. Huntgeburth, *Developing and Evaluating a Cloud Service Relationship Theory*,
Progress in IS, DOI 10.1007/978-3-319-10280-1_1

have enabled the evolution towards cloud computing (Deloitte 2009; Venters and Whitley 2012). The first application service provisioning (ASP) services already existed in the 1990s but did not reach a breakthrough at that time because of immature software and inadequate internet bandwidth on the users' side (Susarla et al. 2003). Just as with ASP services, cloud services offer IT resources as a service over the internet. However, the technological foundations of cloud services are different. In contrast to simple application services, cloud services are massively scalable because they are usually provided on the basis of a collection of connected and virtualized data centers (Armbrust et al. 2010; Iyer and Henderson 2010). Furthermore, the services are provided in different granularities. Infrastructure-services ("infrastructure-as-a-service") provide highly standardized and virtualized computing, storage and network resources, which form the basis for other cloud services. In addition to infrastructure, cloud platforms ("platform-as-a-service") make a development environment from the cloud available to users where they can develop application services ("software-as-a-service"). Two essential models of cloud computing deployment can be distinguished, namely private and public clouds. Private clouds are devoted to a single company only. They may be built, owned, and managed by the organization or by a third party (Mell and Grance 2011). While they offer the highest degree of control over performance, security, and reliability, they are often criticized for being similar to traditional proprietary data centers without the typical advantages of clouds like no up-front capital costs (Zhang et al. 2010). Public cloud services are available to the general public. They are owned, built, and managed by third parties. While there is no fundamental difference in the technical realization compared to private clouds, the user's control over data, network and security is limited.

Within the last years, cloud computing has evolved from a buzzword to a concept that catches the interest of analysts, software vendors, researchers, IT managers and users. While various scholars hype cloud computing as the "long held dream of computing as a utility" (Armbrust et al. 2010) or as a "paradigm shift in the way IT resources are used and distributed" (P.K. Sinha quoted in Greengard 2010), other scholars characterize cloud computing "as a collection of many old and few new concepts" (Youseff et al. 2008) or simply as "an extreme form of IT outsourcing" (Clemons and Chen 2011). In a nutshell, while cloud computing is technically built on many well-established concepts, the cloud movement seems to have the right momentum to impact all important stakeholders—*IT providers*, *IT managers* and *IT users*—and thus, the IT industry as a whole.

From an *IT provider* perspective, the market shares high expectations on the diffusion and adoption of cloud computing (Huntgeburth et al. 2013a). Clouds promise benefits such as lowering capital expenditures and costs, enabling the scalability of computing infrastructure as well as enhancing business (Bain and Company 2012; Boston Consulting Group 2009; Deloitte 2009). The demand for such technological advances is expected to offer new growth markets for IT providers with an overall sales market of $73 billion by 2015 worldwide (Rossbach and Welz 2011). Large software vendors such as SAP and IBM are expanding their cloud business by strategically acquiring innovative cloud service providers.

Example in 2011 SAP bought Success Factors—a company that develops cloud-based employee performance management software—to round up SAP's cloud portfolio (SAP 2011). Other examples include IBM's acquisition of Cast Iron Systems (IBM 2010) or Salesforce's acquisition of Model Metrics (Salesforce 2011). For IT vendors, serving the cloud market represents a shift from a product-centric application model into a globally distributed service-centric provisioning model (Iyer and Henderson 2010). In this new ecosystem, IT providers have to reposition themselves in the IT value chain as infrastructure, service and/or aggregate service providers. Moreover, new and popular subscription and "freemium" revenue models challenge how IT providers' cloud services can turn profitable. While many cloud providers initially focus on establishing a large customer base, they tend to lack a strategy to generate sufficient revenue streams (Travlos 2011).

From an *IT management* perspective, cloud computing can be seen as the high tech trend number one (Bitkom 2012). CEOs worldwide see cloud services as a strategic mean for concentrating on core competencies, enhancing productivity, and enabling simpler solutions for their employees (McAfee 2011). Therefore, they demand that their IT managers fully leverage the opportunities of cloud computing for their company. On the one hand, IT managers can utilize cloud technologies for consolidating or replacing legacy systems (Rossbach and Welz 2011) or for extending their IT software portfolio. Thereby, IT managers can build on previous experience and expertise in outsourcing IT functions (Dibbern et al. 2004). On the other hand, cloud services are supposed to transform the role of the IT department from being an operator, developer and maintainer of IT to an IT facilitator which helps business units to source the best IT resources from the market (McAfee 2011).

From an *IT user* perspective, cloud services empower organizational actors (such as business units or individual users) to design their individual IT architecture in a way that goes beyond what is provided by the IT department (Huntgeburth et al. 2013b). Based on cloud services, employees already build complex and relatively large-scale individually owned-and-operated IT for solving their business problems (Baskerville 2011). Moreover, by making experiences with cloud services in their private life, employees seamlessly transfer and expect these tools in the workplace—a phenomenon called cloud consumerization (Huntgeburth et al. 2013b). Despite strict IT policies, many employees state that they use self-deployed cloud services for solving business problems (36 %) which they often find more useful than the IT products provided by the company's IT function (45 %: survey of 4,017 employees conducted by Accenture 2011). Initially, many enterprises have driven a strategy which involved tight control over the hardware and software used within organizational boundaries. However, these organizations increasingly find it challenging to stay ahead of their tech-savvy employees (Harris et al. 2012). Promising benefits of cloud consumerization such as more productivity, more innovation, and higher user satisfaction have caused IT managers to rethink their consumerization strategies and allow more consumer devices and cloud software enter organizational boundaries.

1.2 IS Research

Since its inception in the 1970s, the IS research discipline has worked on forming a collective identity which helps the community to differentiate itself from purely technological (e.g., computer science) or purely social disciplines (e.g., management science) (Benbasat and Zmud 2003; Hirschheim and Klein 2012). An approach that has helped the IS discipline to build identity and legitimacy is the sociotechnical approach (Sarker et al. 2013). The sociotechnical approach aims for understanding the reciprocal interactions between technical and social subsystems which should—through joint optimization—lead to instrumental (e.g., better performance) and/or humanistic (e.g., higher job satisfaction) goals (Bostrom et al. 2009). While the technical subsystem consists of the business processes and the technologies (hardware and software) needed to support these processes, the social subsystem comprises employees, their skills, values and needs which they bring into the organization (Trist and Murray 1993). The sociotechnical approach provides a perspective on what Zmud and Benbasat (2003, p. 186) have formulated as the core of IS research, namely to understand "[…] (1) how IT artifacts are conceived, constructed, and implemented, (2) how IT artifacts are used, supported, and evolved, and (3) how IT artifacts impact (and are impacted by) the contexts in which they are embedded".

As in any other management and social science research discipline, there is a tension in IS research to fulfill two—often divergent—goals, namely relevance and rigor (Fig. 1.1) (Lee 1999). Practical relevance arises if a research endeavor addresses the needs of organizations and society. Example, cloud success factor research investigates which characteristics a cloud service should exhibit to increase the likelihood that users will adopt a service. The results are useful for IT providers who aim for marketing cloud services. In turn, research projects should aim for systematically advancing the cumulative knowledge about IS. Thereby, rigor is achieved from the effective use of the IS knowledge base—the theoretical foundations and methodological standards for assessing and refining these theories empirically (Hevner et al. 2004). Due to the diversity of epistemological approaches, the nature of theories and methodologies is quite diverse. Gregor's (2006) influential taxonomy of theory types in IS research identifies even five distinct types of theoretical knowledge IS researchers develop ((1) theory for analyzing, (2) theory for explaining, (3) theory for predicting, (4) theory for explaining and predicting, and (5) theory for design and action). Reviewing more than 1,100 articles published in top IS journals, Chen and Hirschheim (2004) identify surveys (41 %), case studies (36 %), laboratory experiments (18 %), field experiments (2 %) and action research (3 %) as the six major methodologies to evaluate and refine IS theories. Consistent to the methodological representation, positivists' hypothetical-deductive method is the dominant epistemological paradigm in IS research (Chen and Hirschheim 2004; Orlikowski and Baroudi 1991).

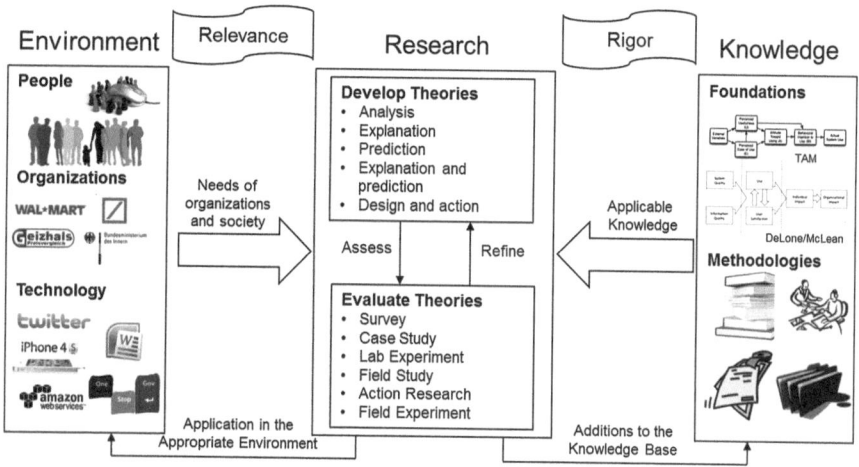

Fig. 1.1 1S research framework (Gregor 2006; Hevner et al. 2004)

1.3 Developing a Framework for Theorizing

Within the last 5 years, IS research has increasingly paid attention to studies examining the changes induced by cloud computing. All leading IS conferences have already devoted tracks for cloud research. Journals such as the European Journal of Information Systems, the Journal of Business Economics and the MIS Quarterly Executive have invited submission for special issues on cloud computing. Cloud research agendas have been proposed in both reputable IS journals (Venters and Whitley 2012) and IS conference proceedings (Ermakova et al. 2013; Ernst and Rothlauf 2012; Huntgeburth et al. 2012). Several theoretical advances on cloud phenomena have been accepted for publication in IS journals (e.g., Benlian et al. 2011; Bhattacherjee and Park 2013; Susarla et al. 2009, 2010). In a nutshell, cloud computing is acknowledged by IS research to change IS practice and the doors for publishing rigorously conducted cloud research are open.

Cloud research distinguishes itself from other reference literature streams, such as IT innovation or IT outsourcing research, through the boundary assumptions about the technical subsystem that individuals or enterprises are exposed to (Bacharach 1989). The motivation to conduct research about cloud computing is in particular the expectation that cloud computing will change the management of IS and that IS theory can only insufficiently explain these changes (Huntgeburth et al. 2012).

During my doctoral studies, I was involved in several cloud research publication projects in which certain experienced-based techniques were rather implicitly used for developing a cloud theory. Central criticisms in the review processes were the questions about (1) why the theory is cloud-specific and (2) how the theory advances the IS knowledge base (cf. Table 1.1 for example reviewer comments).

Table 1.1 Own cloud research projects

Authors	Title	Outlet/ Year	Example anonymous reviewer comment
Huntgeburth, Förderer, Ebertin, Veit	How cloud computing impacts stock market prices	WI 2013	"No explanation is given, why exactly those factors are important to the adoption of cloud computing. Since these factors serve as a basis for the following investigation a more structured approach could have been chosen"
Huntgeburth, Förderer, Veit	Up in the cloud: understanding the chasm between expectations and reality	ICIS 2013	"I would like to recommend the authors to think about the contributions of this paper. The research model is essentially an extension of the EDT by including some cloud computing specific factors. So it is important to beef up the research model and discuss explicitly how this research model contributes to IS research"
Hauff, Huntgeburth, Veit	Exploring uncertainties in a marketplace for cloud computing	JBE 2014	"As already mentioned in the prior review the main critique still refers to the contribution of the article. The author clarification has not shown new insights. It is still difficult to figure out the innovative character of the presented insights"
Trenz, Huntgeburth, Veit	The role of uncertainty in cloud computing continuance	ECIS 2013	"The key findings are interesting, but I am finding it difficult to see the value of many of the findings beyond what has been already reported as concerns in practitioner literature […].. What is unique and interesting from this study that we did not already know? I believe the authors possess this contribution, but it is not conveyed well"

While IS research provides good standards to evaluate what constitutes a theory (Bacharach 1989; Gregor 2006; Whetten 1989), there is only little guidance on how to come to a theoretical contribution. Since IS research is characterized by temporary bursts of interest in new and emerging IT innovations (Baskerville and Myers 2009), the absence of a reflection on theory-building trends in IT innovation research is a little surprising (Colquitt and Zapata-Phelan 2007).

In a nutshell, research on emerging IT innovations such as cloud computing lacks a framework for better carving out the behavioral changes induced by the emerging IT innovation and for developing new perspectives on IT innovation phenomena. This is the first research gap that this dissertation aims to address. Building on the concept of puzzle-solving heuristics (Abbot 2004), recent cloud research is examined with respect to the theory-building practices applied for theorizing about cloud services. Based on the falsificationists' account of science (Kuhn 1962; Popper 1959), these theory-building practices are evaluated and a research framework for theorizing about emerging IT innovations is developed. This intriguing research puzzle-solving idea is summarized in the following research question:

Research Question 1 Which theory-building practices are used by researchers to theorize about emerging IT Innovations and what potential do they contain for advancing IS theory?

1.4 Developing and Evaluating a Cloud Service Relationship Theory

The second part of the dissertation builds on this research framework and develops and evaluates a theory that advances the understanding about an important cloud phenomenon that can only be insufficiently explained by the extant theoretical knowledge about IS. The key sociotechnical enabler of the multifaceted cloud movement described at the beginning is that individuals are willing to continuously depend on a cloud provider and are willing to store as well as process their personal or enterprise data in the cloud. Research on IT user behavior has examined a plentitude of aspects that influence an individual's utilization of IT (Jeyaraj et al. 2006; Venkatesh et al. 2003). However, the shift from IT-as-product to IT-as-a-service implies that the user depends on the provider at all times and has only limited information about the provider's qualities, intentions, and actions. This aspect has been widely neglected in previous research on individual IT user behavior. This is the second research gap that this dissertation addresses.

Through an empirical study of 638 cloud storage users, this dissertation aims to show that agency problems (i.e., moral hazard and adverse selection problems) are prevalent in cloud service relationships. An agency problem occurs if one partner (the principal) delegates work to another (the agent) and the welfare of the principal is affected by the choices of the agent (Jensen and Meckling 1976). Principal-agent theory has been used as a theoretical lens to study uncertainties with regards to search goods (Pavlou et al. 2007) and experience goods (Dimoka et al. 2012) in research on e-commerce transaction. In both cases, the quality of the good can be either evaluated before the purchase decision or upon consumption (Nelson 1970). In contrast, the quality of cloud providers can hardly be evaluated at any point of time since the technological details and the behavior of the provider are hidden from the user. Therefore, cloud services can be best described as credence goods. The user's on-going assessment whether or not to depend on a cloud service, whose quality is hard to discern, puts special emphasis on the importance of uncertainty in this scenario.

Besides studying the role of uncertainty and how uncertainty arises in cloud service relationships, two different types of safeguarding mechanisms that influences users' assessment of the cloud service are examined. The standard account of principal-agent theory proposes that agency problems can be overcome best by signals and incentives (Jensen and Meckling 1976; Milgrom and Roberts 1992). Consistent to this account, bilateral governance mechanisms have been well-established as safeguarding exchange relationships in online environments (Dimoka et al. 2012; Pavlou et al. 2007). In contrast, principal-agent theory is extended by embedding the exchange relationship between cloud provider and user into its social context (Gronevetter 1985). The developed cloud service relationship theory weakens the assumption of agents seeking wealth at the expense of the principal and proposes—complementary to *bilateral safeguarding mechanisms*—*social safeguarding mechanisms* to mitigate uncertainties in cloud service relationships (Wiseman et al. 2012). Further, the goal of this dissertation is to explore contingency factors that influence the explanatory power of the cloud service relationship theory across empirical setting. This intriguing research puzzle-solving idea is summarized in the following research question:

Research Question 2 Why do uncertainties arise in cloud service relationships and how can they be mitigated?

1.5 Expected Contributions of Dissertation

Overall, this dissertation strives to make the following contributions to IS research: From a theoretical perspective, this dissertation systemizes and evaluates cloud research practices and develops based on positivist epistemological assumptions a research framework for advancing theorizing about emerging IT innovations. The framework can be used as a tool by IS researchers for better carving out the behavioral changes induced by emerging IT innovations, for critically assessing own research projects, and for developing new perspectives on IT innovation phenomena.

Leveraging this research framework, a cloud service relationship theory is developed for explaining IT user behavior in cloud service relationships. The cloud service relationship theory extends principal-agent theory using multiple theories. On the one hand, the theory draws on bounded rationality theory and assumes that rationality of cloud users is bounded by the capacity, information and knowledge they have to make decisions. Thereby, the theory assumes that cloud users differ in their aspiration level with respect to a satisfactory cloud service alternative. On the other hand, the theory is developed based on the concept of social embeddedness and assumes that the bilateral economic relationship is embedded in a social context. Therefore, the theory proposes that—complementary to bilateral safeguarding mechanisms of signals and incentives—social influence processes of internalization and identification mitigate agency problems in cloud service relationship scenarios. Using data from cloud storage service users in Germany, the cloud service relationship is finally evaluated.

Besides the theoretical contribution, strong practical implications from the findings are expected for both providers seeking to market their cloud services and IT managers seeking to advocate the uptake of cloud services in organizations. Based on the identified safeguarding mechanisms, providers and IT managers can adjust their strategies to manage the adoption of cloud services.

1.6 Outline of Dissertation

The overall structure and key issues addressed in each chapter are summarized in Table 1.2. This chapter has introduced the background and motivation for this dissertation as well as research questions and expected theoretical contributions.

Table 1.2 Outline of dissertation

#	Title	Key issues
1.	Introduction	Practical motivation of dissertation
		Discipline to which dissertation contributes
		Research gaps the dissertation addresses
		Expected theoretical and practical contributions
2.	A research framework for theorizing	Epistemological foundation
		Overview over cloud research and heuristics used for theorizing
		Development of a research framework for theorizing about emerging IT innovations
3.	Developing a cloud service relationship theory	Motivating the need for a cloud service relationship theory
		Introducing principal-agent theory including concepts such as moral hazard and adverse selection
		Introducing the concept of bounded rationality and social embeddedness
		Development of a cloud service relationship theory
4.	Evaluating a cloud service relationship theory	Scale development
		Survey administration
		Validation of measurement instruments
		Validation of structural model
		Post-hoc analysis of contingency factors
		Discussing key findings, theoretical contribution, limitations, practical implications
5.	Summary and outlook	Answering research questions
		Integrating research framework and cloud service relationship theory
		Presenting overall theoretical and practical contributions of dissertation
		Discussing areas for future research

Chapter 2 provides a reflection and review of cloud research including an overview over and evaluation of theory-building practices. Subsequently, Chap. 3 develops a cloud service relationship theory based on principal-agent theory and the concepts of bounded rationality and social embeddedness. Chapter 4 presents an evaluation of the theory based on an empirical study of cloud storage service users in Germany. Chapter 5 integrates the findings of Chaps. 2–4 and provides an outlook on future cloud research. Each chapter entails title, abstract, content and summary. In order to facilitate the understandability, relevant additional material (such as survey instruments, broader literature analysis etc.) is provided in the appendix.

Chapter 2
A Research Framework for Theorizing

What does it take to have something to say? It takes two things. The first is a puzzle, something about the social world that is odd, unusual, unexpected, or novel. The second is a clever idea that responds to or interprets or solves that puzzle. Everything else—the methods, the literature, the description of data—is really just window dressing. The heart of good work is a puzzle and an idea
Andrew Abbot (2004) in his book "Methods of Discovery: Heuristics for the Social Sciences"

Abstract Every IS researcher applies implicitly (by experience) methods of discovery—so-called heuristics—to advance theorizing about the adoption, the utilization and the success of emerging IT innovations. Heuristics represent experience-based theory-building practices of IS researchers that aim for creating new insights on phenomena. Taking positivist cloud innovation research as an empirical sample, this chapter inductively explores previous cloud research with respect to the heuristics applied and subsequently evaluates—based on positivists' epistemological assumptions—the potential of these heuristics for advancing theorizing and producing scientific progress. The developed research framework can be used as a tool by researchers for better carving out the behavioral changes induced by emerging IT innovations, for critically assessing own research projects, and for developing new perspectives on IT innovation phenomena.

2.1 Introduction

IS research and practice is characterized by temporary waves of interest in new and emerging IT innovations (Baskerville and Myers 2009). These trends are driven by the expectations that these new IT concepts will offer new opportunities for businesses and will sustainably change the management of IS (Fichman 2004). Through empirical studies, IS research aims to examine, e.g., if these new trends will become accepted in practice and which behavioral changes are induced by the IT innovation

© Springer International Publishing Switzerland 2015
J. Huntgeburth, *Developing and Evaluating a Cloud Service Relationship Theory*,
Progress in IS, DOI 10.1007/978-3-319-10280-1_2

(Benbasat and Zmud 2003). In this way, IS research aims to contribute more "objectivity" to the often IT provider-driven hype surrounding new IT concepts and buzzwords. To say it in Andrew Abbot's words: IT innovation research has not a lack of new "puzzles" (e.g., "Why do companies use cloud services?") with respect to emerging IT innovations, rather its challenge is to contribute and advance the theorizing about IT innovation phenomena (Abbot 2004; Hevner et al. 2004) with the help of "clever ideas" (or "Blue Ocean" ideas, see Straub 2009). While IS research provides good standards for evaluating theoretical contributions (Bacharach 1989; Gregor 2006; Whetten 1989), there is only little guidance on the process how to get there. Overall, research on emerging IT innovations such as cloud computing lacks a framework for better carving out the behavioral changes induced by emerging IT innovations and for developing new perspectives on these phenomena.

Like almost no other discipline, IS researchers have strong experiences with investigating the changes induced by technological advances in practice due to the short innovation cycles of the IT industry (Baskerville and Myers 2009). E.g., the rapid proliferation of cloud services is certainly one of the most exciting developments in IS practice in recent years (Armbrust et al. 2010; Venters and Whitley 2012). In the following, cloud services are defined as a virtualization-based style of computing where IT resources are offered in a highly-scalable way as a cloud service over the internet (Sect. 2.2.1 for a more detailed classification) (Huntgeburth et al. 2012). On the one hand, IT executives associate cloud services with technological benefits (Forrest 2009), such as the elimination of upfront investment, low administrative costs, and a more flexible and scalable IT infrastructure (Armbrust et al. 2010; Bain & Company 2012; Forrest 2009). On the other hand, cloud services are seen as a strategic tool for companies to focus more closely on core business competencies, to increase the productivity of business processes, as well as to provide simpler IT solutions for employees (Malladi and Krishnan 2012a).

Compared to previous rather descriptive literature reviews on cloud computing (Ermakova et al. 2013; Ernst and Rothlauf 2012; Huntgeburth et al. 2012; Venters and Whitley 2012), this chapter aims to reflect on previous empirical research on cloud services with respect to the techniques—so called heuristics—used for advancing the understanding of the changes induced by cloud computing. Formally defined, heuristics represent experience-based techniques of IS researchers that aim for creating insights on new phenomena. Every IT innovation researcher uses implicitly (by experience) certain techniques to theorize about emerging IT innovations. Based on the example of cloud innovation research, the literature study attempts to recognize common patterns in recent IS research practices. Finally, the literature study aims to evaluate these patterns with respect to their potential to advance theorizing about emerging IT innovations and to create scientific progress. Due to its partly subjective process, the outcome of the literature review does not aim for providing statistics on how often a heuristic was used. Also the examined articles are not divided into good and bad ones. Rather, this chapter presents a number of heuristics and a research framework which evaluates the heuristics based on epistemological considerations. The resulting framework can be used as a tool by future IT innovation researchers (1) *for better carving out the behavioral changes induced by emerging IT innovations,* (2) *for critically assessing own research projects, and* (3) *for developing new perspectives on IT innovation phenomena.*

The remainder of this chapter is organized as follows. In the next section the characteristics of cloud services are presented. After that, the foundations of heuristics and the epistemological stance are introduced. The first part of the third section introduces the literature analysis method. In the second part of section three, the research framework for theorizing about emerging IT innovations is presented and discussed. The last section sums up and formulates closing remarks.

2.2 Theoretical Foundation

2.2.1 Characteristics of Cloud Services

The idea of cloud services has its origins back in the 1960s, as the vision of "utility computing" was a key driver of the development of the internet (Huntgeburth et al. 2012; Venters and Whitley 2012). A number of technological advances, such as the wide availability of broadband internet, increased processing power of computers, and the increasing standardization of hardware and software, have resulted in the fact that with cloud services the era of IT industrialization has begun (Carr 2003). The first ASP services already existed in the 1990s but did not reach a breakthrough at that time because of immature software and inadequate internet bandwidth on the customers' side (Susarla et al. 2003).

Similar to the first ASP services also cloud services offer IT resources as a service over the internet. Nevertheless, the technological foundations of cloud services are different. In contrast to simple application services, cloud services are massively scalable because they are usually provided on the basis of a collection of connected and virtualized data centers (Huntgeburth et al. 2012). Furthermore, the services are provided in different granularities. Infrastructure-services (*"infrastructure-as-a-service"*) provide highly standardized and virtualized computing, storage and network resources, which form the basis for other cloud services (Armbrust et al. 2010). Additionally to infrastructure, cloud platforms (*"platform-as-a-service"*) make a development environment from the cloud available to users where they can develop application services (*"software-as-a-service"*). Compared to application services of the 1990s, cloud application services are highly standardized, as they are implemented on the basis of the principle of multi-tenancy. In this way, a single instance of a software application can run multiple clients, which brings enormous benefits from the provider perspective for the supply. Since cloud services have similar characteristics as legacy IT service provisioning models (such as ASP), cloud research needs to focus on the unique characteristics of cloud services in order to advance theorizing about cloud phenomena (Armbrust et al. 2010).

2.2.2 *Heuristics*

In mathematics, a heuristic is an *experience-based technique for problem-solving* (Abbot 2004). The most famous work on heuristics was written by the mathematician George Pólya (1945). In his book "How to solve it" he describes four phases of mathematical problem solving: Understanding of the task, devising a plan, executing the plan, retrospection. A large part of the book includes a list of heuristics that introduces procedures to progress from a math problem to a solution.

Such structured approach is very difficult to implement in IS research. An IT innovation research project consists in particular in filtering the aspects which are actually new and interesting about a phenomenon and which have not been investigated in another, related context. Thus, the heuristics of IS research differ from those of mathematics. The challenge of IS research is mainly to explain the changes induced by the emerging IT innovation and to show empirically how previous research lacks explanatory power for explaining these changes. IS researchers apply less concrete problem-solving strategies than in mathematics, but rather use heuristics as a tool (1) *for better carving out original aspects of a phenomenon*, (2) *for critically assessing own research*, and (3) *for developing new ideas and perspectives on a phenomenon* (Abbot 2004). Heuristics therefore have different functions in different phases of a research paper. On the one hand, heuristics, which are based on experience, can be learned and thereby can increase the likelihood that research can produce scientific progress (Straub 2009). On the other hand, heuristics can help to distinguish major and minor theoretical contributions with a certain degree of systemization.

The positivist part of IS research (Chen and Hirschheim 2004; Orlikowski and Baroudi 1991), which will be the focus of the subsequent literature analysis, illustrates the following perspective on scientific progress due to the empirical principle of falsification ("hypothetical-deductive method") (Chalmers 1999). (1) On the one hand scientific theories have to be refutable by an empirical evaluation [demarcation criteria according to Popper (1963)]. (2) Moreover, scientific progress consists primarily in the confirmation of bold conjectures and the rejection of central theories and assumptions of the research paradigm (Kuhn 1962). Publications which confirm bold conjectures signify progress, simply because they mark the discovery of something new, which was not known before or was considered unlikely (Chalmers 1999). The rejection of central theories and assumptions in a study marks a progress, because it determines something as false that was seen as unproblematic. E.g., using a meta-analysis Sharma et al. (2009) show that in empirical studies about IS user behavior the path coefficient between perceived usefulness and use is dependent upon the way how use is empirically measured. The result of that study implies that the outcome of many studies was probably more influenced by the choice of the measuring instrument for use than previously thought ("common method bias"). This is a very important finding for future IS research. The falsification of bold conjectures, as well as the direct application of research models in the "new" context do not provide a significant contribution to

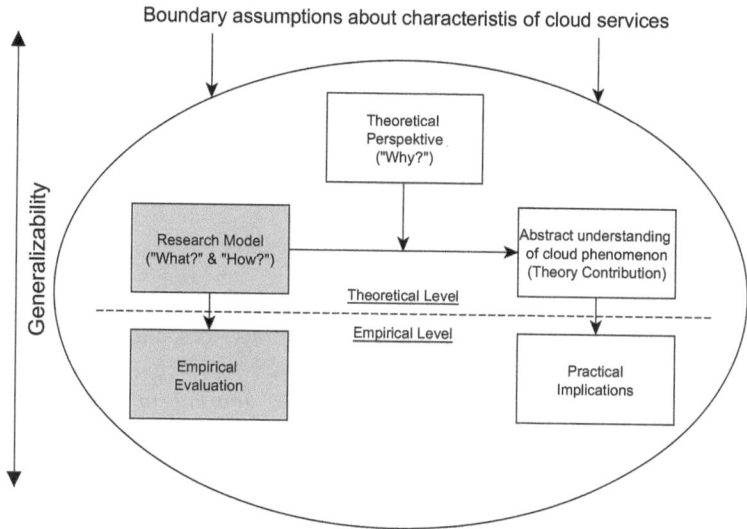

Fig. 2.1 From observations to theory contribution (Bacharach 1989)

research from a falsificationist perspective (for an introduction to falsificationism see: Chalmers (1999).

The boundary assumptions about the unit of analysis distinguish cloud innovation research from other reference literature streams, such as IT innovation or IT outsourcing research (Bacharach 1989). Cloud services have specific characteristics, which distinguish them from other IT innovations, as explained in detail in Sect. 2.2.1. The motivation to produce new research about cloud services is in particular the expectation that cloud services will sustainably change the management of IS and that previous explanation approaches only insufficiently explain these changes (Huntgeburth et al. 2012). In order to develop an abstract understanding of a cloud phenomenon, positivists develop hypotheses derived from a chosen theoretical perspective to explain a given cloud phenomenon (Fig. 2.1).

The proposed research model is then evaluated on the basis of a suitable empirical method (e.g., survey, experiment, case study, etc.). In that case, it must be ensured that the selected empirical context satisfies the boundary assumptions of the theoretical level. This represents a particular challenge of newly emerging IT innovation since certain IT solutions are often called cloud services by practitioners but they actually do not exhibit all the specific characteristics of cloud services (cf. Sect. 2.1). For instance, if "system investment" and "technical integration" are the most important determinants of cloud service continuance, then there might be an inconsistency with respect to the empirical setting in which the research model is evaluated. As low up-front investment and low switching costs represent important characteristics of cloud services, "system investment" and "technical integration" are questionable antecedents of cloud services continuance (Walther et al. 2013c). In the case of a positive evaluation and a successful dissemination, the findings become part of the knowledge base about the management of IS. In addition, implications for practice can be derived from advanced understanding of the cloud phenomenon.

2.3 Structured Literature Review

2.3.1 Methodology

To get an overview of empirical studies on cloud services, the most prestigious journals of the discipline (*European Journal of Information Systems, Information Systems Journal, Information Systems Research, Journal of AIS, Journal of Information Technology, Journal of MIS, Journal of Strategic Information Systems und MIS Quarterly, compare Association for Information Systems 2011*), as well as the conference proceedings of six leading conferences in the field of IS (*International Conference of Information Systems, European Conference of Information Systems, Hawaii International Conference on Systems Sciences, Americas' Conference on Information Systems, Internationale Tagung Wirtschaftsinformatik, Multikonferenz Wirtschaftsinformatik*) were scanned regarding the use of the terms "Cloud", "SaaS", and "Software-as-a-Service" in abstract or title starting from 2007 when the cloud computing hype has been created (criterion (1)). In total, 206 articles were identified (Table 2.1). In the second step, articles which can be assigned to the positivist research paradigm, i.e. only those articles with a behavioral science approach (criterion (2)), a hypothetical-deductive logic (criterion (3)) and an empirical evaluation of the hypotheses (criterion (4)) were chosen. By this selection 36 articles remained, which were subsequently analyzed.

To be deeply familiar with each study, each paper was read in the first step of the second phase of analysis and notes on special features (such as strengths, weaknesses, methods, theoretical perspectives, studied phenomenon) were taken. On the basis of various techniques (e.g.: grouping the papers, paired comparisons of similarities and differences, compare Eisenhardt 1989b) raw categories of heuristics were generated in the second step (Steininger et al. 2011). In the third step, these raw categories were compared with Abbots (2004) heuristics of the social sciences and the relevant literature of positivist theory building and their evaluation (Bacharach 1989; Gregor 2006; Whetten 1989) with the goal of increasing generalizability, strengthening the conceptualization of categories and thereby increasing the theoretical abstraction level (Eisenhardt 1989b). In the last step, all papers were examined a second time to see whether they use one or more heuristics and whether theoretical saturation has occurred in terms of the categories of heuristics. The procedure can be regarded as transparent, but subjective, as the process required a certain degree of judgment and interpretation from the author. The result of the structured literature analysis is thus *no* descriptive statistics on how often a heuristic was used. Likewise, the papers are *not* divided into good and bad ones in

Table 2.1 Overview of the article selection process

Fulfilled criteria	Number of articles									
	Total	EJIS	JIT	MISQ	JMIS	ICIS	ECIS	HICSS	AMCIS	(MK)WI
(1)	206	1	1	1	6	24	26	67	54	33
(1 + 2)	93	1	0	0	3	19	15	12	28	15
(1 + 2 + 3)	51	1	0	0	3	15	9	4	12	7
(1 + 2 + 3 + 4)	36	1	0	0	3	10	9	3	7	3

Abbreviations EJIS European Journal of Irrformation Systems, *JIT* Journal of Information Technology, *JMIS* Journal of Management Information Systems, *ICIS* International Conference of Information Systems, *ECIS* European Conference of Information Systems, *HICSS* Hawaii International Conference on Systems Sciences, *AMCIS* Americas' Conference on Information Systems, *WI* Internationale Tagung Wirtschaftsinformatik, *MKWI* Multikonferenz Wirtschaftsinformatik

the end. Rather, a number of heuristics have been identified and these heuristics—
and not the papers themselves—are examined based on epistemological considerations. The heuristics identified by this method will be presented and evaluated in
the next section. Each heuristic is illustrated by examples from previous cloud
innovation research.

2.3.2 Results

A brief overview about the reviewed articles can be found in Table 2.2. The
structured analysis reveals that 20 studies evaluate hypotheses using a survey, two
with a case study, six with an experiment and eight with secondary data. In the
following, five heuristics are introduced which have been identified throughout the
in-depth literature analysis: "Instantiation", "Laundry-List", "Making an Assumption", "Making an Analogy", and "Challenge the Obvious". These heuristics represent theory-building practices of positivist cloud research. Each heuristics is
illustrated by a prominent example. A more detailed overview over the 36 articles is
provided in Table A.1 in the Appendix.

2.3.2.1 Instantiation

"Instantiation" describes a heuristics for theorizing about emerging IT innovations
that produces new insights by adapting and testing an existing IS research model in a
new empirical setting. Essentially, there are two versions of this heuristic. On the one
hand, there are studies which directly apply well-established hypothesis systems
such as the technology acceptance model ("Perceived Usefulness", "Perceived Ease
of Use", see Bernius and Krönung 2012), institutional theory ("mimetic pressure",
"coercive pressure", "normative pressure", see Kung et al. 2013) or transaction cost
theory ("uncertainty", "specificity", "frequency" Benlian 2009) to the new context.
   As a result, such studies show us that a well-established research model also
applies to the context of cloud services. However, this approach is inconsistent with
the original idea of cloud research, i.e., that cloud services will sustainably change
the delivery of IT and that previous explanatory approaches have only insufficiently
explained these changes (cf. Sect. 2.2.2). On the other hand, authors of several
papers have identified cloud specific sub-dimensions of a theoretical construct, such
as for quality of service (Benlian et al. 2010, 2011) or service success (Walther et al.
2013a, b, c) and tested these sub-dimensions in the new cloud context (cf. also
example in Fig. 2.2). In practice, these cloud specific sub-dimensions are useful
because evaluation indicators for the management of cloud services can be derived
from these models. The potential of this strategy to advance theorizing, however,
remains limited because no new theoretical insights can arise from this heuristic.
Also Abbot (2004) proposes that this "more-of-the-same heuristic" has its
limitations:

Table 2.2 Structured literature analysis

#	Autor (Year)	Outlet	Survey	Case study	Experiment	Secondary data
1	Huang and Wang (2009)	ICIS				X
2	Benlian (2009)	ECIS	X			
3	Susarla et al. (2009)	JMIS	X			
4	Benlian and Hess (2009)	WI	X			
5	Benlian and Hess (2010)	ECIS	X			
6	Koehler et al. (2010a)	AMCIS			X	
7	Ramireddy et al. (2010)	AMCIS		X		
8	Koehler et al. (2010b)	ICIS			X	
9	Saya et al. (2010)	ICIS	X			
10	Benlian et al. (2010)	ICIS	X			
11	Susarla et al. (2010)	JMIS	X			
12	Lehmann et al. (2010)	MKWI			X	
13	Winkler et al. (2011)	ICIS		X		
14	Parameswaran et al. (2011)	AMCIS				X
15	Sun and Wang (2012)	ICIS				X
16	Winkler and Benlian (2012)	ICIS	X			
17	Li and Chang (2012)	AMCIS	X			
18	Malladi and Krishnan (2012b)	AMCIS				X
19	Bernius and Krönung (2012)	ECIS	X			
20	Opitz et al. (2012)	HICSS	X			
21	Retana et al. (2012)	ICIS				X
22	Malladi and Krishnan (2012a)	ICIS				X
23	Ackermann et al. (2012)	ICIS	X			
24	Benlian et al. (2011)	JMIS	X			
25	Kim et al. (2013)	ECIS				X
26	Walther et al. (2013b)	AMCIS	X			
27	Kung et al. (2013)	AMCIS	X			
28	Lansing et al. (2013)	ECIS			X	
29	Walterbusch et al. (2013)	ECIS			X	
30	Walther et al. (2013a)	ECIS	X			
31	Walther et al. (2013c)	ECIS	X			
32	Trenz et al. (2013)	ECIS	X			
33	Bhattacherjee and Park (2013)	EJIS	X			
34	Coursaris et al. (2013)	HICSS	X			

(continued)

Table 2.2 (continued)

#	Autor (Year)	Outlet	Survey	Case study	Experiment	Secondary data
35	Borgman et al. (2013)	HICSS			X	
36	Huntgeburth et al. (2013a)	WI				X
	Overall		20	2	6	8

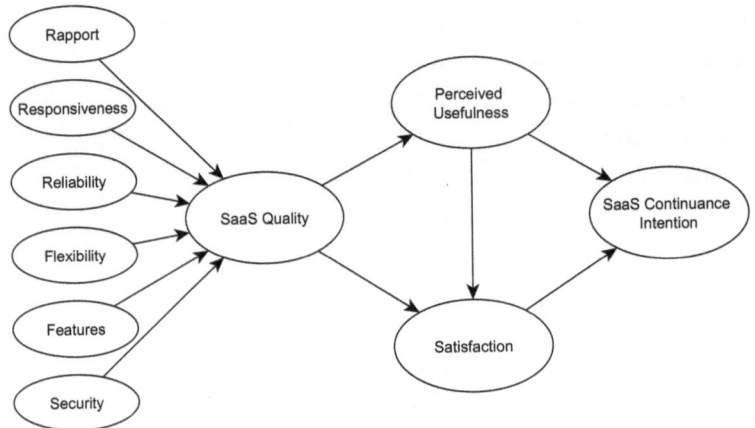

Fig. 2.2 "Instantiation": quality dimensions for cloud (Benlian et al. 2011)

Adding new cases or variables or rules is always a useful first step in the full evolution of ideas. And so it is right and fitting that most of us begin our careers with the additive heuristic, and it is not at all surprising that many of us never leave it. But the ultimate aim of heuristic is to improve on such normal science. [...] Invention is what we seek, not just addition. (Abbot 2004, pp. 91–92)

2.3.2.2 Laundry-List

The "Laundry-List" approach (also called "pick-and-choose-approach") describes a heuristic for theorizing about emerging IT innovations, in which a research model is developed in absence of a coherent theoretical perspective. The vast majority of success factors research can also be ascribed to the "Laundry-List" heuristic. In cloud research, manifestations of this heuristics can be found in the fields of adoption decision-making (Borgman et al. 2013; Coursaris et al. 2013) or user behavior (Li and Chang 2012), which test the influence of well-established success factors in this "new" theoretical context without a coherent theoretical framework (cf. also example in Fig. 2.3). As explained in Sect. 2.2.2, an essential part of a theory is an explanation of "which" theoretical constructs are relevant, "how" they

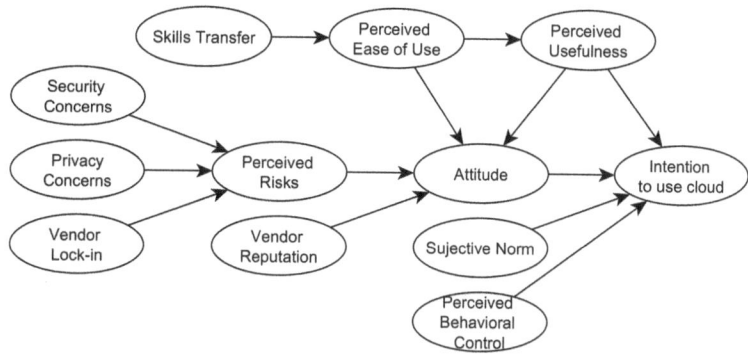

Fig. 2.3 "Laundry-List": explains cloud acceptance (Li and Chang 2012)

are related and "why" (Whetten 1989). In falsificationism, the whole theoretical perspective should be evaluated by the empirical observations and not just each success factors individually (Bacharach 1989; Whetten 1989). While from a practical point of view the "Laundry-List" can be used to derive recommendations for cloud providers, the potential of the "Laundry-List" to advance theorizing about emerging IT innovations remains very limited.

2.3.2.3 Making an Assumption

With the help of the "Making an Assumption" heuristic new insights about cloud phenomena can be gained by making an assumption that a new aspect plays a significant role in the cloud context. There are two characteristics of this heuristic in research on cloud services. On the one hand, there are studies about cloud guarantees (Lansing et al. 2013), user risk perceptions (Benlian and Hess 2010) or trust in cloud (Walterbusch et al. 2013), which assume, without empirical verification, that these aspects influence the behavior of actors (suppliers, customers) and elaborate on this aspect in detail. On the other hand, there are studies which attempt to integrate this "new aspect" into the nomological network of previous research to highlight the importance of this "new aspect" empirically (Benlian and Hess 2010; Trenz et al. 2013).

E.g., cloud computing eliminates an up-front commitment by cloud users allowing them to start small and increase or reduce computing resources as needed (Armbrust et al. 2010). This also implies that market success for cloud providers depends on consumers' post-adoption rather than adoption behavior. Therefore, many cloud studies focus on continuance as a dependent variable (Benlian et al. 2010, 2011; Trenz et al. 2013; Walther et al. 2013a, b). Moreover, cloud users are highly dependent on the provider over the whole-life cycle of the business relationship. Therefore, the characteristics of the cloud provider-user relationship (e.g., goal conflict, fears of opportunism, information asymmetry, cf. Jensen and

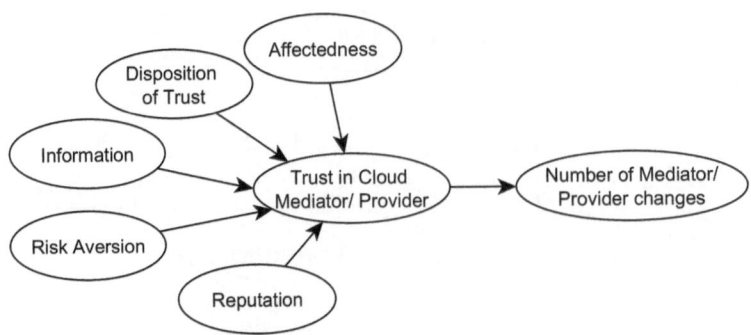

Fig. 2.4 "Making an assumption": trust in cloud (Walterbusch et al. 2013)

Meckling 1976) have to be incorporated when studying user-related issues of cloud computing. Therefore, several studies focus on relational aspects between provider and user (cf. example in Fig. 2.4). As the special characteristics of cloud services are made exogenous in research models, the "Making an Assumption" heuristic has the potential to advance theorizing about emerging IT innovation and produce scientific progress.

2.3.2.4 Making an Analogy

The "Making an Analogy" heuristic describes a technique that advances theorizing about cloud phenomena by using theoretical perspectives of distinct research areas for theory development. A convincing application of this heuristic is the study of Bhattacherjee and Park (2013), who make an analogy between the migration from hosted to cloud solutions and the migration of people into new geographic locations. Based on the theory of migration ("A Theory of Migration") different "pull"-, "push"—and "mooring"—mechanisms are identified (cf. also example in Fig. 2.5). The "Making an Analogy" heuristic has its advantage in the fact that theorizing can utilize the ideas of researchers who have been thinking about a similar problem in a completely different context. The "Making an Analogy" heuristic should not be confused with the "Instantiation" heuristic. The "Making an Analogy" heuristic borrows only the theoretical perspective from another (IS) research field. In comparison, the "Instantiation" heuristic directly applies well-established hypotheses that do not go beyond what was known before in the field of IT innovation research.

2.3.2.5 Challenge the Obvious

The "Challenge the Obvious" heuristic describes a technique that advances theorizing about cloud phenomena by showing that well-established hypotheses do not apply in the context of cloud services. A number of cloud studies show that

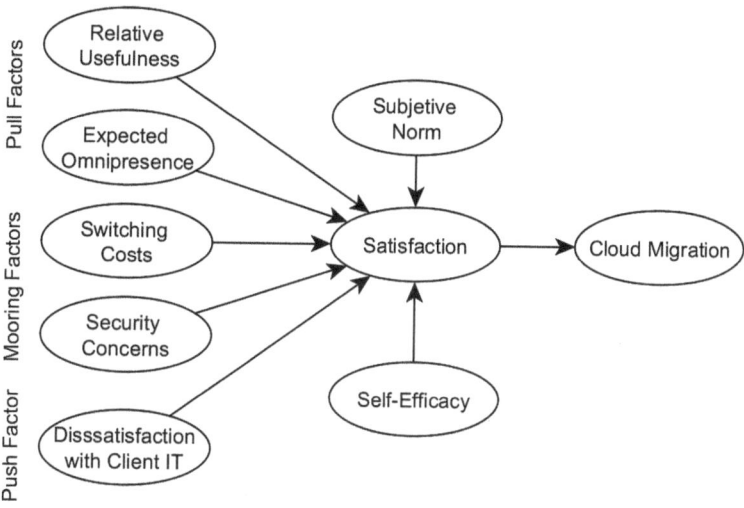

Fig. 2.5 "Making an analogy": migration (Bhattacherjee and Park 2013)

well-established explanatory models, such as institutional theory (Kung et al. 2013), IS success model (Walther et al. 2013a) or transaction cost theory (Benlian 2009) do not apply for explaining behavior for certain groups (cf. also example in Fig. 2.6). They demonstrate this empirically by using group comparisons in the empirical evaluation and show that the validity of the model is contingent on contextual factors. E.g., Winkler et al. (2011) show that successful governance of cloud services is dependent on various application-specific contingency factors (Dibbern et al. 2008). The weak point of the previous applications of this heuristic in the cloud area is the lack of reference to cloud-specific contingency factors (Kung et al. 2013; Walther et al. 2013b). Since contingency factors describe the degree to which the research model can be generalized (cf. boundary assumptions, Sect. 2.2.2), contingency factors should describe the user context or the perceived characteristics of the cloud service.

Fig. 2.6 "Challenge the obvious": institutional theory (Kung et al. 2013)

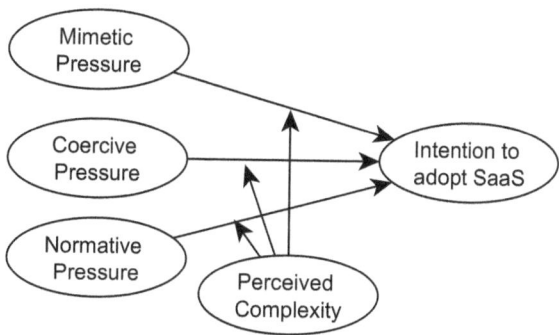

2.3.3 Discussion

In falsificationism, scientific progress arises through the confirmation of bold conjectures and the rejection of central theories and assumptions of the research paradigm (cf. Sect. 2.2.2). For the heuristics introduced, one can tendentially say which heuristics have the highest potential to advance theorizing about emerging IT innovations and create scientific progress (Table 2.3). The "Instantiation" and "Laundry-List" heuristics essentially use well-established knowledge about IS and test this knowledge in a new empirical context. The potential of these heuristics to create new insights is thus very limited. "Challenge the Obvious" has principally the potential to put existing knowledge about IS into question. The challenge of this heuristic is that the findings must be considered in relation to established theories. A weakness of the previous applications of this heuristic in cloud research is a lack of explanation why established theories do not apply in the context of cloud services. The heuristics "Making an Assumption" and "Making an Analogy" probably offer the greatest potential for research on new and innovative IT artefacts because they take the characteristics of cloud services into account and provide new perspectives on cloud phenomena. Even if Karl Popper wrote in his early works of falsificationism that a rejection of a bold conjecture represents scientific progress ("naive falsificationism", see Chalmers 1999), this perspective has not established itself with a good reason. As Chalmers (1999, p. 80) already remarked "[...] ... if a bold conjecture is falsified, then all that is learned is that yet another crazy idea has been proven wrong".

A number of remarks have to be made regarding the presented research framework for theorizing about emerging IT innovations (Table 2.3). The framework is developed on the basis of post-positivist assumptions: ontological realism, possibility of an objective truth, and creating new insights based on the hypothetical-deductive method (Chen and Hirschheim 2004). The framework was developed exploratory on the basis of 36 articles, Abbot's (2004) heuristics of social sciences, and the relevant literature on positivist theory construction and their evaluation (Bacharach 1989; Eisenhardt 1989b; Gregor 2006; Whetten 1989). More work is needed to understand if there are additional heuristics that are commonly used for the examination of emerging IT innovations and these additional heuristics have to be evaluated based on epistemological considerations. Also more sub-dimensions of the heuristics should be included to strengthen the practical use of the

Table 2.3 A research framework for theorizing

		Theoretical level	
		Bold conjecture	Cautious conjecture
Empirical level	Confirmed	"Making an assumption"	"Instantiation"
		"Making an analogy"	"Laundry-list"
	Falsified	–	"Challenge the obvious"

framework for researchers. Each researcher uses implicitly (by experience) heuristics. This work represents a first attempt to make a systematization of heuristics that can be used for theorizing about emerging IT innovations.

2.4 Summary

While IS research provides good standards to evaluate what constitutes a theory (Bacharach 1989; Gregor 2006; Whetten 1989), there is only little guidance on the process of theorizing about emerging IT innovations if at all. Every IS researcher applies implicitly heuristics to advance theorizing about the adoption, the utilization and the success of emerging IT innovations. This chapter has reviewed theory-building practices in cloud innovation research and has—based on epistemological assumptions—developed a framework for theorizing about emerging IT innovations out of it (Table 2.3). The framework will be leveraged in the following chapter to develop a cloud service relationship theory.

Summary

Chapter 3
Developing a Cloud Service Relationship Theory

> *Created within the context of specified boundaries and built from abstract constructs or their more concrete manifestations (variables), theoretical systems take the form of propositions and proposition-derived hypotheses. While both propositions and hypotheses are merely statements of relationships, propositions are the more abstract and all-encompassing of the two, and therefore relate the more abstract constructs to each other. Hypotheses are the more concrete and operational statements of these broad relationships and are therefore built from specific variables.*
> Samuel B. Bacharach (1989) in the Academy of Management Review.

Abstract This chapter develops a cloud service relationship theory that explains and predicts how uncertainties arise and how they can be mitigated in cloud service relationships. In the first part, the relevance and boundary assumption of the theory are explained. Next, based on well-established theoretical lenses, an abstract understanding of user behavior in cloud service relationships is developed. Building on these more abstract constructs and their relationships, empirically testable hypotheses are derived. By the end of this chapter, a summary of the essential elements of the theory is provided.

3.1 Boundary Assumptions

3.1.1 Practical Relevance

Cloud computing is a disruptive technology that redefines how IT markets offer (Bain and Company 2012), IT departments manage (Deloitte 2009) and users consume IT (Armbrust et al. 2010; Harris et al. 2012). While analysts propose that worldwide cloud service revenues are set to triple to nearly $73 billion by 2015 (Rossbach and Welz 2011), IT providers are gradually positioning themselves as IT utility providers to their customers (Armbrust et al. 2010). With cloud services, IT departments can transform their enterprise IT infrastructure from a product-centric to a globally distributed, agile, service-centric model (Iyer and Henderson 2010). Thereby, enterprises can move away from traditional software deployment

© Springer International Publishing Switzerland 2015
J. Huntgeburth, *Developing and Evaluating a Cloud Service Relationship Theory*,
Progress in IS, DOI 10.1007/978-3-319-10280-1_3

paradigms—where IT adoption and use are promoted from the management level down—to a diffusion and innovation model, where business units and end-users promote the utilization of innovative software services (Deloitte 2009).

> Cloud computing is empowering, as anyone in any part of world with internet connection and a credit card can run and manage applications in the state of the art global datacenters; companies leveraging cloud will be able to innovate cheaper and faster.
> Jamal Mazhar (2010), Founder and CEO - Kaavo

As a result, cloud services have the potential to empower organizational actors (such as entire business units or individual users) to redesign their individual IT infrastructure in a way that goes beyond what is offered by the organizational IT department. At the same time, cloud services blur the boundaries between private and enterprise IT work systems (Baskerville 2011). The representative empirical study presented in the next chapter reveals that at least half of the German internet users already store business and private data in the public cloud—a trend that is expected to continue. Moreover, many employees declare to use self-deployed IT for solving business problems which they often find more useful than the IT products provided by the company's IT function (Accenture 2011). Based on cloud services and privately-owned consumer devices, employees build already complex and relatively large-scaled IT infrastructures for solving their business problems (Baskerville 2011). Considering individual level advantages such as more productivity, more innovation and more end-user satisfaction, IT consumerization strategists recommend enterprises to 'broadening the scope' or even 'advocating the controlled uptake' of bottom-up cloud service adoption processes to fully leverage the opportunities of cloud computing for the company (Harris et al. 2012).

In the light of these revolutionary changes in IT practice, *cloud service relationships* become more and more ubiquitous. A *cloud service relationship* is a bilateral economic exchange between a cloud user and a cloud provider based on a standardized service level agreement (SLA). Figure 3.1 depicts a typical cloud service relationship. The cloud provider offers highly standardized service to a crowd of cloud users. A subset of the cloud user's social peers may also maintain a cloud service relationship with the cloud provider. Embedded in a social network, standardized interfaces allow cloud users to exchange information with their social peers if they use the same or a compatible cloud service (Iyer and Henderson 2010).

3.1.2 Theoretical Relevance

From a theoretical perspective, cloud services represent a shift from IT-as-a-product to IT-as-a-service (Iyer and Henderson 2010). In contrast to IT product scenarios where IT users are relatively independent from the IT provider once they have deployed the software, cloud users continuously depend on the cloud provider (Benlian et al. 2011). While IT products typically allow users to keep all personal or enterprise data on the enterprise's infrastructure, cloud users entrust their data to a shared public infrastructure hosted by the cloud provider (Armbrust et al. 2010).

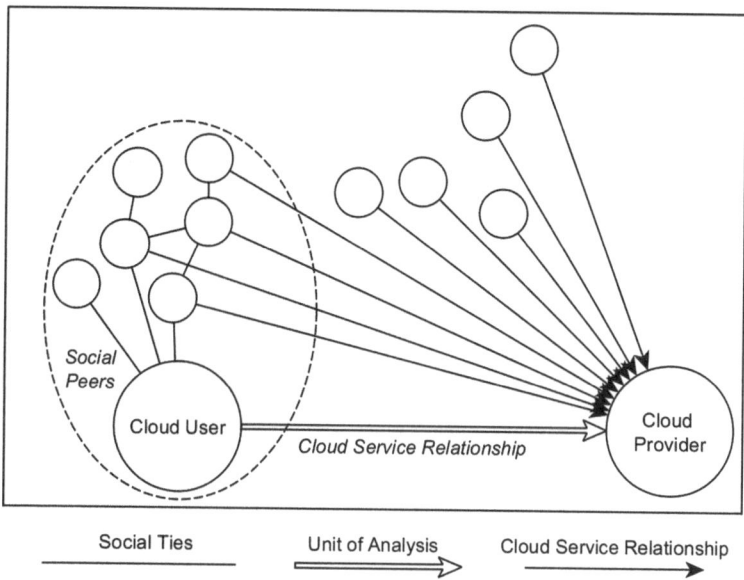

Fig. 3.1 Cloud service relationships

Research on IT user behavior has examined a plentitude of aspects that influence individual's evaluation and utilization of IT often assuming an organizational top-down adoption model (Fichman 2004). Thereby, functional (e.g., performance and effort expectancy), organizational (e.g., top management support, user support, social norms) or more recently motivational (e.g., perceived locus of causality) aspects have been shown to be the best predictors of individual's utilization of IT (Jeyaraj et al. 2006; Malhotra et al. 2008; Venkatesh et al. 2003). However, an aspect that becomes important for explaining user behavior in cloud service relationships has been widely neglected in IT adoption theory.

> Concerns about cloud security have grown in the past few years. In 2009, the fear was abstract: a general concern, as there is with all new technologies when they're introduced. Today, however, concerns are both more specific and more weighty. We see cloud users placing a lot more scrutiny on cloud providers as to their controls and security processes, and they are more likely to defer adoption because of security inadequacies than to go ahead despite them. Jonathan Penn (2010), analyst at Forrester Research

The shift from IT-as-a-product to IT-as-a-service implies that the user depends on the provider at all times and has only limited information about the cloud provider's qualities and actions. User's on-going assessment whether or not to depend on a cloud service whose quality is hard to discern puts special emphasis on the importance of understanding the consequences, antecedents and mitigators of cloud users' uncertainty in this scenario. Drawing on principal-agent theory and the concepts of bounded rationality and social embeddedness, this chapter presents a cloud service relationship theory that explains how cloud users' uncertainties arise in cloud service relationships and how they can be mitigated.

3.2 Propositions

3.2.1 Principal-Agent Theory

The principal-agent perspective is a well-established theoretical lens to study bilateral-economic relationships where goal congruence and information asymmetries exist (Milgrom and Roberts 1992). Agency relationships can be observed in all kinds of economic transactions such as employment relationships (Jensen and Meckling 1976), medical care (Arrow 1963) or spot market exchanges (Akerlof 1970). In IS research, principal-agent theory has also been applied to a variety of IS research phenomena such as IT outsourcing (Dibbern et al. 2004), e–commerce transactions (Dimoka et al. 2012; Pavlou et al. 2007) or software project development (Keil et al. 2000a).

Principal-agent theory explains why economic transactions take place in a situation where one self-interested partner (the principal) delegates work to another self-interested partner (the agent) and where information asymmetries between the partners exist (cp. Fig. 3.2). Agency problems can arise from two sources: (1) *Adverse selection* appears whenever the principal has hidden information about the agent's true qualities (Akerlof 1970). In this situation, principals face a pool of potential transaction partners and cannot easily discriminate between high-quality and low-quality agents. (2) *Moral hazard* arises once the principal decides to rely on the agent and the agent does not perform as promised or engage in hidden actions at the principal's expense (Jensen and Meckling 1976).

The cloud service relationship theory assumes that agency problems (*adverse selection* and *moral hazard*) are also prevalent in cloud service relationships. The user delegates its data to the cloud provider and depends on the cloud service over the whole life-cycle of the business relationship. The cloud provider and the user have different interests and goals. For example, cloud users want a high-quality service, whereas providers want to operate their service at the lowest expense possible and want to earn revenues. Cloud services can be best described as credence goods, i.e., it is impossible for the user to fully verify the provider's true qualities or fully monitor provider's actions. For example, there can be a significant time lag until users recognize reduction in promised service quality. In some case (e.g. selling critical information to competitors), the hidden actions of the provider

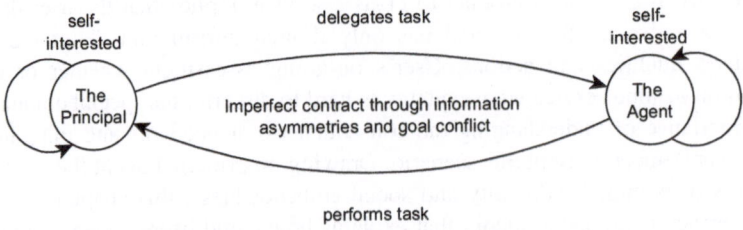

Fig. 3.2 The principal-agent relationship

may even never been detected. *Adverse selection* and *moral hazard* are distinct, concurrent and persistent problems in cloud service relationships since the quality and actions of the cloud provider can never be fully evaluated. Both agency problems can never be fully resolved and stay persistent. Thus, a first proposition is formulated:

Proposition 1 Moral hazard and adverse selection are distinct, concurrent and persistent agency problems in cloud service relationships and influence cloud users' utilization of the cloud provider's services.

Positivist agency theorists are primarily interested in the governance mechanisms that safeguard economic transactions between the principal and the agent (Eisenhardt 1989a). The standard account of principal-agent theory proposes that the best means to overcome agency problems are *signals* and *incentives* (Jensen and Meckling 1976; Milgrom and Roberts 1992). *Signals* and *incentives* are bilateral governance mechanisms between a cloud user and its cloud provider. *Signals* are designed and sent by the cloud provider (the agent) to disclose private information about its true qualities to the cloud user (the principal) (Spence 1973). In turn, *incentives* are used to align the interests of the cloud provider (the principal) and the cloud user (the agent) and therefore, make opportunisms or hidden actions of the cloud provider (the principal) costly. Accordingly, it is assumed that both *signals* and *incentives* mitigate agency problems in cloud service relationships. Therefore, it is formally proposed:

Proposition 2 Bilateral safeguarding mechanisms (signals and incentives) mitigate agency problems in cloud service relationships.

3.2.2 Bounded Rationality Theory

The principal-agent perspective assumes that agent and principal act in self-interest and rational, i.e., both gather and process all relevant information for making optimal choices (Jensen and Meckling 1976; Milgrom and Roberts 1992). This "rational man" assumption has been widely criticized for having only limited accuracy for explaining human behavior (Sen 1977). Given that cloud services are complex technologies and the potential utility or value of using them is hard to predict, the assumption that cloud users always expend the full effort required to evaluate alternatives is rather inaccurate for individual IS decision-making.

A more accurate decision model for the context of cloud service relationships is developed by Herbert Simon who assumes that individuals are limited by the capabilities, knowledge and information they have and therefore use heuristics for solving complex decision-making problems (Simon 1955). Simon's *bounded rationality* theory proposes that individuals examine alternatives sequentially and select the first *satisfactory alternative* instead of evaluating the full set of potential alternatives. This behavior is termed satisficing.

The concept of *bounded rationality* also applies to cloud service relationships where cloud users have different capabilities, knowledge and information about cloud services leading to different aspiration levels with respect to a satisfactory cloud service alternative. If cloud users have a high aspiration level, agency problems are stronger considered in decision-making; in contrast, for cloud users with low aspiration level, the influence of agency problems on the utilization of cloud services is mitigated. Consequently, it is formally proposed:

Proposition 3 Cloud users' rationality is bounded by the aspiration level they have on a satisfactory cloud service alternative.

3.2.3 Social Influence Theory

Another criticism of the classical account of principal-agent theory is that it does not take the social context of the exchange relationship into account thereby limiting the theory's validity outside a specific context in which agents maximize economic wealth and shirk their responsibilities (Davis et al. 1997). However, earlier research has highlighted that this is not a problem of principal-agent theory but rather an opportunity to extend the theory by formally incorporating a social perspective into the theory (Gronevetter 1985; Wiseman et al. 2012). Wiseman et al. (2012) proposes that the higher the density of a social network surrounding principal-agent relationships, the more likely principals will defer to their social network for assessing agent's quality and monitoring agent's behavior.

Following their view, the cloud service relationship theory assumes that cloud user-provider relationships are embedded in a social structure that shapes users' evaluation of the cloud provider's qualities and actions. The social context is particularly important in cloud service relationships since the qualities and actions of the cloud provider can never be fully monitored by the cloud user directly (credence good). Therefore, social influence processes are introduced in the following that complement bilateral safeguarding mechanisms (signals and incentives) in cloud service relationships.

Cloud users' evaluation of the service is shaped in important ways by the social world in which they reside (Schmitz and Fulk 1991). Social influence theory suggests three processes—*compliance, internalization* and *identification*—through which individuals' attitudes, beliefs and behavior are influenced (Kelman 1961). *Compliance* processes develop if individuals accept influence from social peers because they hope to achieve a favorable reaction from the others (Fishbein and Ajzen 1975). In this scenario, the evaluation of a technology and consequent behavior might be in conflict because individuals act according to social norms rather than their own beliefs. While this form of social influence has been well-established to explain user behavior (Venkatesh et al. 2003), social peers do not adjust their evaluation of a technology based on the social world in which they reside unless they internalize others' opinion. Therefore, compliance-based social influence processes do not play a role for explaining cloud users' evaluation of the cloud service.

In contrast, *identification* and *internalization* are social influence processes in which others' opinions become more and more internalized into individuals' own value system (Kelman 1961; Wang et al. 2013). Previous research on IT user behavior shows that these social influence processes—compared to compliance-based processes—persist over time and particularly influence ongoing experience with and use of technology (Thompson et al. 1991; Venkatesh and Morris 2000). *Identification* occurs when individuals *identify* with their social peers and as a result adopt believes, attitudes and behaviors (Kelman 1961). *Internalization* occurs when individuals *internalize* others' opinions and act in accordance with these opinions (Malhotra and Galetta 2005).

Therefore, social influence processes of *internalization* and *identification* are assumed to shape in important ways how individuals evaluate agency problems in cloud service relationships (Wang et al. 2013). Cloud users incorporate social peers' opinions into their own evaluation of the cloud service (*internalization*) as well as observe important others' behavior and incorporate this into their own evaluation of the service (*identification*). Cloud users' evaluation of agency problems is thus likely be shaped by social influence processes of *internalization* and *identification*. Therefore, it is formally proposed:

Proposition 4 Social influence mechanisms (internalization and identification) mitigate agency problems in cloud service relationships.

The cloud service relationship theory combines principal-agent, bounded rationality and social influence theory to explain cloud user behavior in cloud service relationships (abstract understanding depicted in Fig. 3.3). First, adverse selection and moral hazard were proposed to influence the cloud user's utilization of the cloud service, while signals and incentives were assumed to be means for overcoming these agency problems. Second, challenging the assertion of principal-agent theory that all principal decide fully informed and rational, it was proposed that

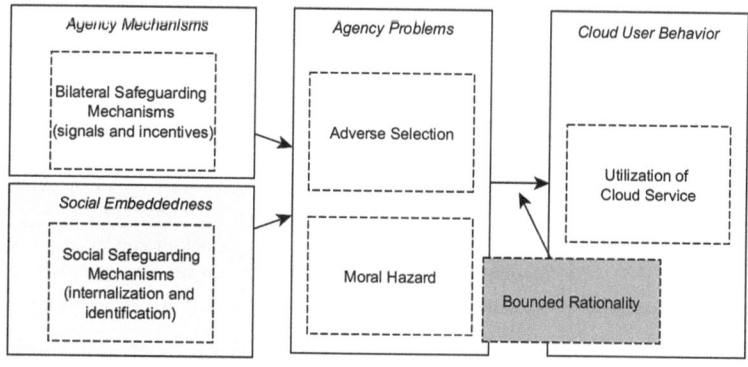

Fig. 3.3 A cloud service relationship theory (propositions-level)

cloud users' behavior is bounded by the aspiration level they have on a satisfactory cloud service alternative. Finally, having considered that users are embedded in a social network, it was suggested that identification-based and internalization-based social influence processes complement bilateral mechanisms in safeguarding cloud service relationships. Since one building block of a theory is empirical testable hypotheses (Bacharach 1989), more concrete manifestations of the theoretical construct are developed in the following section.

3.3 Hypotheses

3.3.1 Agency Problems

Practitioner literature sources are reviewed to identify instantiations of agency problems in this new theoretical context (Accenture 2010; Bain and Company 2012; Boston Consulting Group 2009; Burton Group 2009; Deloitte 2009; Deutsche Bank Research 2012; Ernst and Young 2011; Gartner 2008; KPMG 2010; PWC 2013). Overall, five distinct concerns are identified that IT users and managers have with adopting and using cloud services: security, privacy, availability, provider viability and lock-in concerns. These concerns are categorized with respect to the agency problem to which the concern can be best attributed (adverse selection versus moral hazard) as well as whether the concern is specific to cloud services (cloud-specific concerns) or whether the concern applies to any type of IT (general concerns) (Table 3.1). Since the goal is to develop a comprehensive, parsimonious and cloud-specific theory (Bacharach 1989), provider viability and lock-in concerns are not integrated into the nomological network of the cloud service relationship theory as explained in more detail below.

Because the cloud is a virtual environment and data can be located anywhere, the most important reasons for avoiding online transactions are not linked to functionality but are related to users' loss of control over their data (data-related concern) (Hoffman et al. 1999). *Security* and *privacy* concerns are shown to be two major obstacles for users to engage in online exchange environments (Pavlou et al. 2007). Security concerns arise because cloud services are provided over a publicly shared infrastructure causing considerable vulnerabilities.

Table 3.1 Cloud users' manifestations of agency problems

	Adverse selection	Moral hazard
General concerns	Provider viability concerns (*dependency-related*)	Lock-in concerns (*dependency-related*)
Cloud-specific concerns	Availability concerns (*dependency-related*)	Privacy concerns (*data-related*)
	Security concerns (*data-related*)	

> Culture and comfort aside, simply communicating data over the public internet [...] may increase data vulnerability. In addition, the business models of cloud service providers involve sharing infrastructure among many clients [...] The shared infrastructure issue effectively links the security fates of all users in a given cloud in a sort of unintended commune (Ernst and Young 2011, p. 26).

Security concerns are defined as the user's belief about the cloud provider's ability to safeguard users' personal information from security breaches during transmission and storage (Salisbury et al. 2001). Due to information asymmetries, the cloud user can hardly judge whether security breaches occur and whether the appropriate prevention measures are in place (*adverse selection*) (KPMG 2010). Depending on the evaluation of cloud providers' security qualities, cloud users are more or less willing to use cloud services (Deloitte 2009). Therefore, it is formally proposed:

Hypotheses 1a Cloud user's perceived security concerns (adverse selection) will negatively influence her or his intention to [continue to] use the cloud provider's service (utilization of cloud services).

Privacy concerns are defined as cloud user's evaluation of the likelihood of unauthorized secondary use or disclosure of her or his data to third parties without the user's consent (Kim 2008). Leaked by former National Security Agency (NSA) contractor Edward Snowden, reports on internet surveillance programs such as PRISM, XKeyscore, or Temporta reveal that privacy protection is very often unattended for reasons of national security (Der Spiegel 2013).

> Taken together, the revelations have brought to light a global surveillance system that cast off many of its historical restraints after the attacks of Sept. 11, 2001. Secret legal authorities empowered the NSA to sweep in the telephone, internet and location records of whole populations (Gellman 2013).

Since data is accessed via the internet, the disclosures have reinforced cloud users' and IT managers' privacy concerns (The Guardian 2013). Cloud users particularly fear surveillance from legal authorities, competitive intelligence or other secondary use of their personal or business data (Ernst and Young 2011). Due to information asymmetries, cloud users can hardly assess whether the cloud provider engages in any hidden actions related to secondary use or disclosing data without cloud users' consent (*moral hazard*). Thereby, the question of whether this behavior is opportunistic (i.e., the provider acts in economic self-interest) or not (i. e., the provider is legally forced to act by an authority) does not play a role for the user's evaluation. Depending on the evaluation of cloud provider's privacy protection practices, cloud users are more or less willing to use the service. Therefore, it is formally proposed:

Hypotheses 1b Cloud user's perceived privacy concerns (moral hazard) will negatively influence her or his intention to [continue to] use the cloud provider's service (utilization of cloud services).

Besides concerns that can be attributed to users' loss of control over their data, users' concerns can also arise from the commitment to and resulting dependence on the cloud provider's service (Deutsche Bank Research 2012). In order to rely on a cloud provider, cloud users expect a reliable uptime of the cloud service (Bitcurrent 2011). *Service availability concerns* refer to the user's beliefs about a cloud provider's ability to deliver a high level of service uptime. Due to information asymmetries, the user can hardly evaluate whether the cloud provider has sufficient resources and capacity to guarantee a high level of service availability (*adverse selection*). *Service availability concerns* are particularly salient if the cloud service is used for supporting users' critical business processes. Prior research has highlighted the important role of reliability on the overall performance evaluation of IT service users (Susarla et al. 2003). Depending on the evaluation of cloud provider's service availability qualities, cloud users are more or less willing to use the service. Therefore, it is formally proposed:

Hypotheses 1c Cloud user's perceived service availability concerns (adverse selection) will negatively influence her or his intention to [continue to] use the cloud provider's service (utilization of cloud services).

Apart from service availability, the dependency-related concerns also arise by users' anticipated cost for switching the cloud provider. For cloud users, switching the service involves among others retrieving the data from the cloud provider and uploading it to the new service as well as adapting business processes to the functionalities of the alternative cloud service (Deutsche Bank Research 2012). Moreover, switching costs for cloud users can be of social nature (Jones et al. 2007), for instance reflected in the lost benefit of exchanging data with other users of the same service. Therefore, *lock-in concerns* are defined as the provider's unwillingness to provide service terms and interfaces that allow users to easily switch to other providers without any economic losses (Zhu et al. 2006b). Switching costs economics have been intensively examined in previous research because these concerns similarly arise when users adopt and use IT products (Shapiro and Varian 1999). As the primary interest of the study is to understand cloud-specific concerns, *lock-in concerns* are not incorporated in in the cloud service relationship theory.

Finally, with many emerging players in the cloud market, providers' business viability is a concern for users, especially with provider consolidation expected in the coming years (Deloitte 2009). If a cloud service provider goes out of business, users are rarely able to retain the effective use of their data, e.g., including the collaboration options with peers. Therefore, *provider viability concerns* are defined as the cloud user's belief about the ability of the provider to continue service provisioning (adverse selection). Due to information asymmetries, cloud users can hardly judge whether the cloud provider has sufficient user network growth, loyalty and revenue streams needed for the viability of the cloud service (Travlos 2011). Just like lock-in concerns, provider viability concerns also arise when users adopt and use IT products, e.g., because of future security updates and advancements of the product that break down if IT providers run out of business. They might be particularly pronounced when users face high switching costs. Again, since the study only focuses on cloud-specific concerns to theoretically manifest agency problems, provider viability concerns are not incorporated in the cloud service relationship theory. Table 3.1 provides an overview of cloud users' manifestation of agency problems and again highlights (grey cells) the focus of the theory development.

3.3.2 Bounded Rationality

A limitation of Simon's (1955) initial work is that he did not elaborate on why individuals satisfice, i.e., why they spend less cognitive effort in decision-making. Since one can hardly measure cloud users' aspiration level directly, proxy variables are used for categorizing respondents into cloud users with low and high aspiration level on a satisfactory cloud service. Drawing on ideas of contextual rationality (Krosnick 1991; March 1978), it is assumed that the latent aspiration level is a function of two factors, namely the cloud user's knowledge about cloud technology and the cloud user's interest in alternative cloud services. Cloud users who possess high knowledge about and interest in alternative cloud service find it easier and are more strongly motivated to optimize, i.e., to evaluate the full set of cloud service alternatives (Krosnick 1991; Krosnick et al. 1996).

Consequently, the cloud service relationship theory assumes that cloud users who lack knowledge about and interest in (alternative) cloud services tend to have a lower aspiration level on a satisfactory cloud service alternative and therefore, take cloud-specific concerns less strongly under consideration (Table 3.2). In turn, cloud users with high attentiveness to cloud service alternatives and high cloud knowledge tend to have a higher aspiration level on a satisfactory cloud service alternative and incorporate their concerns more strongly into their decision-making.

Attentiveness to alternatives is an important behavioral variable in marketing and has also been used as an outcome variable in previous IS studies (Bendapudi and Berry 1997). It refers to cloud user's lack of interest in alternative cloud services (Kim and Son 2009). Cloud knowledge refers to the degree to which users believe that they are knowledgeable about cloud services. The cloud service relationship theory assumes that both knowledge and interest are necessary conditions for users to evaluate the full set of alternative cloud services and thus take a rational choice. Therefore, it is formally proposed:

Table 3.2 Characterizing cloud users with high and low aspiration level

Type of users		
High aspiration level	High interest in alternative cloud services	High knowledge about cloud services
Low aspiration level	Low interest in alternative cloud services	Low knowledge about cloud services

Hypotheses 2 The less knowledge about cloud services a cloud user has (bounded rationality), the weaker the relationships between users' perceived (a) security (adverse selection), (b) privacy (moral hazard) as well as (c) availability concerns (adverse selection) and users' intention to [continue to] use the cloud provider's service (utilization of cloud services).

Hypotheses 3 The less interest in alternative cloud services a cloud user has (bounded rationality), the weaker the relationships between users' (a) perceived security (adverse selection), (b) privacy (moral hazard) as well as (c) availability concerns (adverse selection) and users' intention to [continue to] use the cloud provider's service (utilization of cloud services).

3.3.3 Bilateral Safeguarding Mechanisms

The role of signals for safeguarding economic exchanges has been well-established in IS and marketing research (Dimoka et al. 2012; Pavlou et al. 2007; Susarla et al. 2003). Information signals assist cloud users to evaluate the quality of a cloud service, thereby facilitating decision making (Crawford and Sobel 1982; Rao and Monroe 1989). While there is no perfect correspondence between signaling investments and their evaluation by cloud users (Pavlou et al. 2007; Singh and Sirdeshmukh 2000), this study aims to examine the information signals that are used—on average—most by cloud users and thus mitigate agency problems (Dimoka et al. 2012).

Product diagnosticity and third-party assurance are well-established information signals for safeguarding online exchange environments (Dimoka et al. 2012; Pavlou et al. 2007). The concepts of website informativeness and product diagnosticity— the degree to which users believe that a website provides them with useful information about the respective product (Jiang and Benbasat 2004; Kempf and Smith 1998)—are extended to the context of cloud service relationships. Cloud service diagnosticity thus refers to user's belief about the ability of cloud provider's website to convey relevant information that can assist the user in evaluating the cloud service. Thus, a visible and clear website helps users to evaluate the service and thus, mitigates agency problems:

Hypothesis 4 Perceived cloud service diagnosticity (signal) will negatively influence users' (a) perceived security (adverse selection), (b) privacy (moral hazard) and (c) availability concerns (adverse selection).

In contrast to a website, third-party assurances are differentially costly and utilize the credibility of a third party to mitigate quality concerns. Differently costly means that signals are differently costly for low and high quality cloud providers.

Differentially costly is the most important property of information signals because effective signals must induce signaling costs. In other words, it should be more costly for bad [cloud providers] to transmit the signal [...], and it must be more costly for bad [cloud providers] than good ones to transmit a signal [...]. If these two properties are satisfied, [cloud users] should be able to rely on signals to distinguish across [cloud providers] (Dimoka et al. 2012, pp. 9–10)

Third-party assurances refer to user's belief that the cloud provider possesses credible assurances from third-party institutions. Third-party assurances are expected to be effective information signals that cloud users can rely on. If cloud providers do not provide these credentials, cloud users may deduce that cloud providers possess hidden information about their true qualities and actions. Moreover, cloud providers with lower qualities are expected to have more effort in hiding low quality from credited third-party institutions. Therefore, third-party assurances are costly and credible information signals that effectively mitigate agency problems:

Hypothesis 5 Perceived third-party assurance (signal) will negatively influence users' (a) perceived security (adverse selection), (b) privacy (moral hazard) and (c) availability concerns (adverse selection).

Apart from information signals, there are also mechanisms that align the interest of principal and agent making opportunism costly (i.e., incentives). Cloud service relationships are typically protected by service level agreements (SLAs) (Buyya et al. 2008). Cloud-SLAs are formal written contractual agreements between the cloud user and the cloud provider that specify the various facets of the service to be provided (Goo et al. 2009). As cloud services are credence goods and users cannot fully monitor the performance of the cloud provider, cloud-SLAs rarely entail any financial rewards for providers meeting service level agreements. Rather legal sanctions (e.g., punishment for SLA violations) are a mean to make opportunistic behavior of the cloud provider costly (Gefen et al. 2008). Accordingly, *legal sanctions*, defined as the user's perception of the severity of punishment if the cloud service violates the SLAs, are bilateral governance mechanisms that can foster the alignment of users' and cloud providers' interest (Peace et al. 2003). The higher the legal sanctions of violating SLAs are, the higher are the incentives for cloud providers to meet the promised service level. Therefore, it is formally proposed:

Hypothesis 6 Perceived legal sanctions (incentive) will negatively influence users' perceived (a) security (adverse selection), (b) privacy (moral hazard) and (c) availability concerns (adverse selection).

3.3.4 Social Safeguarding Mechanisms

Social influence processes of both identification and internalization operate through two different channels: verbal communication and nonverbal interaction (Rogers 2003; Wang et al. 2013). Via internalization processes, cloud users incorporate the opinion of social peers into their own value system (Kelman 1961). Thus, internalization-based social influence processes mostly operate through verbal communication between social peers. In contrast, identification mostly operates through non-verbal interaction, i.e., cloud users seek to believe and act in a similar manner like social peers (Wang et al. 2013). Via internalization, users' cognition about the expected outcome of cloud service use is influenced by the behavior of social peers (Lewis et al. 2003).

Compared to IT products, cloud services are often promoted through a "word-of-mouth model, where user community opinion leaders promote the software adoption through peer evangelization" (Deloitte 2009, p. 55). WOM is an important behavioral variable in marketing (de Matos and Rossi 2008; Mangold et al. 1999) and IS research (Kim and Son 2009). From a social influence theory perspective, word-of-mouth (WOM) activities of social peers influence cloud users' personal norms and how they evaluate cloud services (Malhotra and Galetta 2005). WOM influence refers to any informal communication between the cloud user and its social peers concerning the evaluation of a service (Anderson 1998). WOM influence on cloud users can be both positive and negative. Previous research has highlighted that users place different weights on these distinct influence processes in making evaluations (Richins 1983). Therefore, it is postulated that cloud users internalize WOM influence of both positive and negative valence into their evaluation of the cloud service:

Hypothesis 7 Perceived positive WOM influence (internalization) will negatively influence users' (a) perceived security concerns (adverse selection), (b) privacy concerns (moral hazard) and (c) availability concerns (adverse selection).

Hypothesis 8 Perceived negative WOM influence (internalization) will positively influence users' (a) perceived security concerns (adverse selection), (b) privacy concerns (moral hazard) and (c) availability concerns (adverse selection).

Besides internalizing social peers' opinions into their own value system, cloud users evaluation is also shaped by non-verbal communication. Via identification, cloud users seek to believe and act in a manner similar to those possessing referent power (Lewis et al. 2003). It is proposed that peer adoption—defined as the extent to which social peers have adopted the service (Zhu et al. 2006b)—influences cloud users' evaluation of the service. Cloud users are eager to build social capital, which makes them sensitive not only to what others say but also what others do (Eagly and Wood 1982; Wang et al. 2013). Consequently, non-verbal interaction among social peers—in the form of adoption behavior—influences how cloud users evaluate the service:

Hypothesis 9 Perceived peer adoption (identification) will negatively influence users' perceived (a) security concerns (adverse selection), (b) privacy concerns (moral hazard) and (c) availability concerns (adverse selection).

3.4 Summary

The overall research model is depicted in Fig. 3.4. The cloud service relationship exhibits all components of a theory (cf. citation from the beginning of chapter). First, the boundary assumptions of the theory were explained. Second, an abstract

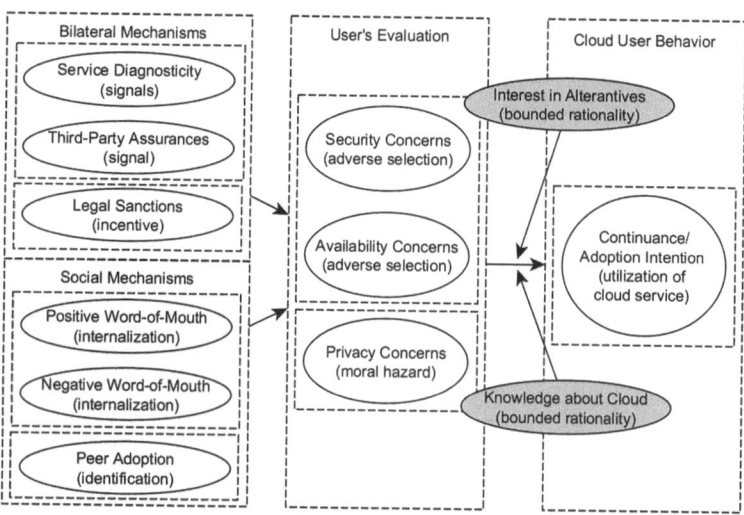

Fig. 3.4 A cloud service relationship theory (hypotheses-level)

understanding of the cloud service relationship theory in the form of proposition was developed. Principal-agent theory was extended using the concepts of bounded rationality (Simon 1955) and social embeddedness (Gronevetter 1985). These extensions are believed to increase the theory's explanatory power and predictive ability for the new theoretical context. Third, operational manifestations of the key theoretical constructs were derived from academic and practitioner literature.

A positive assessment of the theory expects to make the following three theoretical contributions. First, the study aims to show that agency problems are prevalent in cloud service relationships. Second, the study seeks to show that rationality of cloud users is bounded by the capacity, information and knowledge they have to make decisions. Thereby, it is assumed that cloud users differ in their aspiration level with respect to a satisfactory cloud service alternative. Third, going beyond principal-agent theory, the cloud service relationship theory assumes that the bilateral economic relationship is embedded in a social context. Therefore, the study aims to show that—complementary to bilateral safeguarding mechanisms of signals and incentives—social influence processes of internalization and identification mitigate agency problems in cloud service relationship scenarios.

The theory is also highly relevant for practice. On the one hand, IT departments can understand in which situations cloud users' concerns are taken under consideration for their decision-making and how the evaluation process is shaped by social and bilateral safeguarding mechanisms. On the other hand, the theory can help providers to successfully manage their customers' uncertainties by understanding the mechanisms involved in mitigating cloud users' concerns. However, since one cannot contribute to theory if the hypotheses are not tested with observations (Popper 1959), an empirical evaluation of the cloud service relationship theory is presented in the next chapter.

Chapter 4
Evaluating a Cloud Service Relationship Theory

Bold ideas, unjustified anticipations, and speculative thought, are our only means for interpreting nature: our only organon, our only instrument, for grasping her. And we must hazard them to win our prize. Those among us who are unwilling to expose their ideas to the hazard of refutation do not take part in the scientific game.
Karl Popper (1959) *in his book* "The Logic of Scientific Inquiry"

Abstract This chapter presents an empirical evaluation of the cloud service relationship theory based on a large scale survey. First, the context in which the cloud service relationship was evaluated is introduced and an explanation is given why PLS-SEM was chosen as a statistical method. Second, a comprehensive scale development study is presented that was very valuable for developing reliable and valid measurement instruments. Third, transparent record is provided on the sampling strategy and how the survey was administered. Fourth, the results of both measurement model and structural model evaluation are presented. Fifth, the findings are discussed in the light of the extant knowledge about IS and the theoretical contribution of the study is carved out. Last but not least, implications for practice are provided and limitations of the empirical evaluation are debated.

4.1 Introduction

4.1.1 Study Context

Finding an empirical context for evaluating the cloud service relationship theory was a difficult endeavor. Since the diffusion and adoption of cloud services is still at the beginning, only a few cloud services exist which are widely adopted by internet users and which are used within and beyond enterprise boundaries. Moreover, many providers claim to offer cloud services but these application scenarios often do not share the typical characteristics of cloud services such as scalable IT resources and no up-front commitment (Armbrust et al. 2010).

© Springer International Publishing Switzerland 2015
J. Huntgeburth, *Developing and Evaluating a Cloud Service Relationship Theory*,
Progress in IS, DOI 10.1007/978-3-319-10280-1_4

Based on these requirements, cloud storage services were identified as a suitable empirical context for testing the cloud service relationship theory. Cloud storage services such as Dropbox, Google Drive or Microsoft SkyDrive allow cloud users to back-up, synchronize and share their files over the internet (Armbrust et al. 2010). They are widely adopted by internet users and share the typical characteristics of clouds. Moreover, the relationships between users and providers can be perfectly described as cloud service relationships (cf. previous chapter). Corresponding, users of cloud storage services can never fully evaluate the qualities and actions of the cloud storage provider.

4.1.2 PLS-SEM versus CB-SEM

A well-established statistical method for testing theoretical systems is structural equation modelling (SEM). Second-generation multivariate analysis techniques like SEM allow researchers to study relationships between unobservable variables (*latent variables*) indirectly measured by indicator variables (*items*) most often obtained based on survey data (Chin 1998). The major advantage of SEM compared to linear regression models is that it allows researchers to simultaneously assess the measurement instruments (*measurement model*) for each latent variable and the relationships among the variables (*structural model*) (Gefen et al. 2011), thereby allowing to account for *measurement errors* (Chin 1998). SEM has been one of the most frequently applied methods in IS research (Chen and Hirschheim 2004; Ringle et al. 2012).

Two different types of SEM approaches exist, covariance-based SEM (CB-SEM) and partial least square SEM (PLS-SEM), which differ in their underlying philosophy and estimation objectives (Gefen et al. 2011). On the one hand, CB-SEM emphasizes how well the proposed research model account for measurement item co-variances, thereby offering various indices how well parameter estimates match sample co-variances (Chin 1998). On the other hand, PLS-SEM uses the empirical data for estimating relationships with the aim to maximize the explained variance in the endogenous latent variable (Hair et al. 2014). The primarily goal is therefore to predict and explain variance.

There is an ongoing controversial debate about which SEM tool to use as well as CB-SEM's and PLS-SEM's relative ability to support the empirical evaluation of hypothesized relationships among variables (Goodhue et al. 2006, 2012; Marcoulides et al. 2012). Two popular reasons for choosing PLS-SEM were that it provides more accurate results for studies with small sample sizes and non-normally distributed variables (Ringle et al. 2012). However, this assertion has not been confirmed by previous comparison studies.

Rather, a recent Monte Carlo simulation-based study of Goodhue et al. (2012) shows that CB-SEM and PLS-SEM provide consistent results regarding testing relationships between variables:

[…] if one is in the early stages of a research investigation and is concerned more with identifying potential relationships than the magnitude of those relationships, then regression or PLS would be appropriate. As the research stream progresses and accuracy of the estimates becomes more important, LISREL (or other CB-SEM techniques) would likely be preferable (Goodhue et al. 2012, p. 999).

To sum the discourse up, the choice of the SEM should primarily depend on the research objective. Thereby, PLS-SEM is more suitable for exploratory and CB-SEM is more suitable for explanatory evaluations of theoretical systems. Given the early stage of the investigation, the exploratory character of the study and the primary interest in identifying potential relationships between variables, PLS-SEM was decided to be used for evaluating the cloud service relationship theory. However, consistent empirical results are expected when using CB-SEM.

The PLS-SEM algorithm follows a two-stage approach to estimate path coefficients (Henseler et al. 2012). Because this is necessary for understanding the evaluation approach, the operating principles of the PLS-SEM algorithm are described in the following using the path model example depicted in Fig. 4.1.

In the first stage the variable scores (Y1–Y3) are iteratively estimated based on the empirical data. This stage consists of four steps which are repeated until the sum of the outer weights' (W1–W6) changes drops a defined limit. Outer weights are initially set to 1. In the first step, the observed item values and the outer weights (W1–W6, from step 4) are used to compute the latent variable scores (Y1–Y3) (outer approximation of latent variable scores). Second, the PLS-SEM algorithm computes the path estimates (P1, P2) using the path weighting scheme which maximizes the final R^2 value estimations of the dependent variable (Y3) (Lohmöller 1989). Third, the latent variable scores of the dependent variable (Y'3) are calculated based on the latent variables scores from step one (Y1–Y2) and the path estimates from step two (P1, P2) (inner approximation of latent variable scores). Fourth, the outer weights (W1–W6) are calculated based on the correlations between the inner proxy of each latent construct from step three (Y'1 to Y'3) and the observed item values. Once the first stage terminates, outer loadings (W1–W6) as well as path coefficients (P1–P2) and the resulting explained variance of the endogenous latent variables (R^2 value) are finally estimated using the ordinary least squares method (cf. Henseler et al. (2012) for more details).

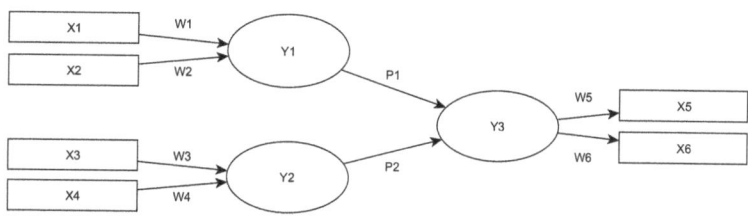

Fig. 4.1 Path model example (Hair et al. 2011)

4.1.3 Structure of Chapter

After having introduced the statistical method for evaluating the cloud service relationship theory, the next section presents how the measurement instruments have been developed and pre-validated. Section three provides details on the process of data collection including how the online survey has been administered and how the study controls for satisficing behavior of respondents. Section four present the results of the measurement model and structural model evaluation as well as several sub sample comparisons. The key findings and theoretical results are discussed in section five. Finally, section six sums the insights gained up.

4.2 Scale Development Study

The goal of the scale development study was to develop and refine the measurement models for all latent variables used in the empirical study. In this process, the study followed the guidelines recommended by MacKenzie et al. (2011) who propose the following steps to develop and refine measurement models: (1) developing a conceptual definition of the latent variables, (2) generate items that represent the latent variables and qualitatively assess the content validity of the items, (3) formally specify the measurement model, (4) collect data to conduct a pre-test, and (5) refine scales for the final measurement models used in the main study.

4.2.1 Conceptual Definition of Variables

Poor variable conceptualizations can have severe consequences on the validity of the empirical evaluation (MacKenzie 2003). If latent variables are poorly conceptualized, it is difficult for the researcher (1) to develop multiple measures that represent the latent variable's domain, (2) to correctly specify how the variable relates to its measure, and (3) to provide a strong rationale for hypotheses (linking the latent variables). Also poor conceptualization could result in invalid conclusions because hypotheses have to be rejected because the measures are not capturing what they are supposed to capture (MacKenzie et al. 2011).

In order to develop strong conceptual definitions of the variables, previous research and practitioner studies were examined with respect to how the variables have been defined (Benlian et al. 2011). Most of the operational manifestations that were developed in the previous chapter were identified based on academic and practitioner literature. Therefore, finding clear and concise variable definitions was based on these sources. Second, the nature of each latent variable's conceptual domain was specified by identifying the type of property the variable represents and the entity to which it applies (Sartori 1984). Finally, each variable was checked whether it only captures one or multiple dimensions and whether the latent variable is stable over time and across situations (MacKenzie et al. 2011). As a result, 12 clear and concise conceptual definitions were developed that define each variable in unambiguous terms (Table 4.1).

4.2.2 Qualitatively Assessment of Content Validity

SEM researchers use multiple measures for each variable to …

> [...] (a) better capture the full domain of complex [variables] (Churchill 1979), (b) un-confound the method of measurement from the [variable] of interest (Campbell and Fiske 1959), and (c) enhance the reliability of measurement (Nunnally 1978) (MacKenzie 2003, pp. 323–324).

Table 4.1 Conceptual definition of each variable

Variable	Conceptual definition
Continuance intention (CONT)	Users' intention to continue using the cloud service (Bhattacherjee 2001)
Perceived security concerns (SEC)	User's belief about the cloud provider's ability to safeguard personal data from security breaches during transmission and storage (Salisbury et al. 2001)
Perceived privacy concerns (PRIV)	User's belief about the likelihood of unauthorized secondary use or disclosure of her or his data to third parties without consent (Kim 2008)
Perceived availability concerns (AVA)	User's belief about cloud provider's ability to deliver high level of service uptime
Perceived service diagnosticity (DIA)	User's belief about a cloud provider website's ability to convey relevant information that can assist in evaluating the service (Jiang and Benbasat 2007)
Perceived third-party assurance (TPA)	User's belief that the cloud provider possesses credible assurances from third-party institutions (Dimoka et al. 2012)
Perceived legal sanctions (LS)	User's perception of the severity of punishment if the cloud service violates the SLAs (Peace et al. 2003)
Perceived positive WOM influence (PWOM)	Positive informal communication between the cloud user and its social peers concerning the evaluation of a service (Anderson 1998)
Perceived negative WOM influence (NWOM)	Negative informal communication between the cloud user and its social peers concerning the evaluation of a service (Anderson 1998)
Perceived peer adoption (PAD)	Extent to which social peers have adopted the service (Zhu et al. 2006a)
Knowledge about cloud (KNOW)	Degree to which users believe that they are knowledgeable about cloud services
Attentiveness to alternatives (ATT)	User's lack of interest in alternative cloud services (Kim and Son 2009)

Table 4.2 Example of item rating

Rater number = 1	SEC	PRIV	AVA
Item #1: I am concerned that Dropbox could be temporarily unavailable when I need it	1	1	5
Item #2: I am concerned that Dropbox is collecting too much information about me	2	5	1
Item #3: I feel safe in making transactions on Dropbox	4	1	1
...	...	...	...
Item #n: I feel secure in transferring information when using Dropbox	5	1	1

Moreover, multiple measures allow accounting for measurement errors as explained later on. The objective of the initial item creation and qualitative evaluation process was to ensure content validity. Content validity refers to the extent to which multiple measures represent all facets of a given theoretical variable (Moore and Benbasat 1991).

First, a variable search engine[1] and previous studies using similar variables were utilized to create an initial pool of items. Where needed, additional items were developed based on practitioner literature and expert interviews. The goal was to develop at least six items per latent variable allowing erasing and modifying items at a later stage of the measurement development and evaluation process.

Because respondents are Germans, two colleagues independently translated all variable definitions and corresponding items into German language (Benlian et al. 2011). These translations were consolidated into one translation. Subsequently, a third colleague re-translated the variables and items into English language. This step allowed verifying whether items lost their original meaning through the translation. In several cases, the German translation was adapted again to avoid any loss of meaning.

Third, the recommendations of MacKenzie (2011) were followed to qualitatively assess the content validity of each set of item. For each area of the theoretical system (cloud user behavior, user's evaluation, bilateral mechanisms, social mechanisms, see previous chapter), a matrix was prepared in which conceptual definitions of each variable was listed at the top of the columns and the corresponding items in the rows (cf. an example for all variables related to 'user's evaluation of the cloud service' in Table 4.2). Thereby, items were randomly assigned to a row. Next, two raters rated the extent to which each item captured the domain of each variable in the column. The raters were asked to use a scale ranging from 1 (does not capture the variable domain) to 5 (does fully capture the variable domain). By the end, each item was analyzed across the raters' evaluation.

---

[1] Inter-nomological network scale search engine covering IS, marketing and psychology studies operated by the Human Behavior Project at the Leeds School of Business, http://inn.colorado.edu/.

Subsequently, items were modified or deleted which captured no or more than two domains of different variables. By the end, the measures exhibited both content and discriminant validity (i.e., each item only measures one latent variable).

4.2.3 Formal Specification of Measurement Models

Previous simulation studies show that poorly specified measurement models can bias structural parameters estimates (Jarvis et al. 2003; MacKenzie et al. 2005; Petter et al. 2007). Therefore, considerable attention was spent in formally specifying the measurement models. Two types of measurement models can be distinguished. With *reflective measurement* models, changes in the latent variable causes changes in the measures, whereas changes in the measures cause changes in the variable with *formative measurement models* (Hair et al. 2014; Petter et al. 2007). It is important to note that latent variables are not inherently formative or reflective in nature (MacKenzie et al. 2011). Rather, it depends on the items and the conceptualization of the variable, whether a measurement model can be characterized as reflective or formative.

The decision rules proposed by Jarvis et al. (2003) were used to evaluate whether the measurement models are reflective or formative. Finally, all tentative measurement models were assessed as reflective since (1) changes in the variable would have caused changes in the items, (2) items had similar content and dropping an item would not have altered the domain of the variable, (3) items were strongly correlated with each other, and (4) the nomological network for the items did not differ (Petter et al. 2007).

4.2.4 Data Collection for Pre-test

In order to refine the measurement instruments, a pre-test was conducted using survey data from PhD candidates, master and bachelor students of a German university. Students represent an important segment of German internet users and have widely adopted cloud storage services. Therefore, this group was assessed as a useful subsample of the whole population of cloud storage service users. After inviting these candidates via a social networking site, 112 responses were collected of which 89 declared to use Dropbox as a cloud storage service. For these 89 students the survey was customized to answering questions about their experience with Dropbox.

4.2.5 Scale Refinement and Purification

The objective of the scale development study was to reduce the measurement error, i.e., to minimize the difference between the true value of the variable and the value obtained by the measurement (Mooi and Sarstedt 2011). Formally the true value equals the measured value plus the measurement error (Hair et al. 2014). In turn, the measurement error is composed of a systematic error (threatening validity), and a random error (threatening reliability). The difference between reliability and validity can be explained by the illustration depicted in Fig. 4.2. Each rounded circle depicts a measurement of one latent variable, whereas the cross represents the average value of the circles. *Validity* and *reliability* can be assessed in the following manner: On the one hand, the closer the circles are to the cross, the higher is the reliability of the measurement model. E.g., the measures of the targets at the top are reliable because there is only a small *random error* in the measurement model, i.e., the circles are all close to the average measurement. On the other hand, the closer the cross to the center of the target, the higher is the *validity* of the measurement model. E.g., the targets on the left are not valid because the measures exhibit a *systematic error*, i.e., on average they do not measure what they are supposed to measure. For measurement models, reliability is a necessary condition for validity because without reliable measures, one cannot differentiate between systematic and random error (Hair et al. 2014; Mooi and Sarstedt 2011), i.e., if one would repeat the measurement another five times, the random error would shift the cross to a different position on the target. For reflective measurement models in PLS-SEM, there are three criteria for evaluating the reliability and validity of the measurement

Fig. 4.2 Comparing reliability and validity (Mooi and Sarstedt 2011)

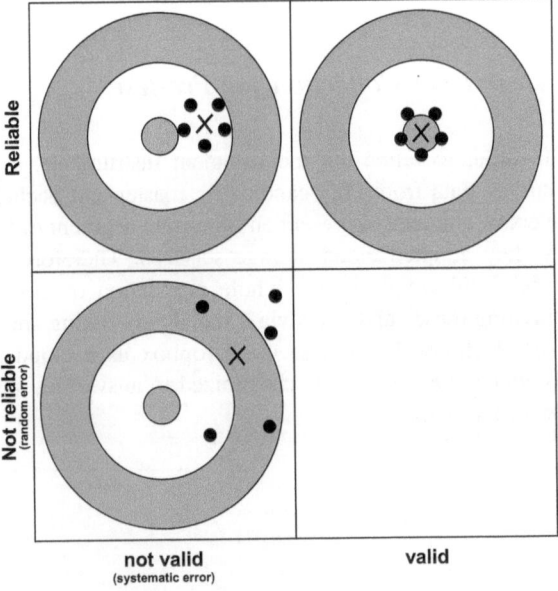

models, namely *internal consistency reliability, convergent validity* and *discriminant validity* (Henseler et al. 2009). The final measurement models were modified and refined based on these criteria and the pre-test data.

Internal consistency reliability assures that items which are supposed to measure the same latent variable are all strongly correlated with the latent variable (Henseler et al. 2009). In PLS-SEM, *internal consistency reliability* is assessed based on the *composite reliability* score. Compared to Cronbach's alpha which assumes that all items have equal correlations with the latent variable (i.e., equal outer loadings) (Cronbach 1951), composite reliability takes the different correlations between the items and the latent variable score into account (Werts et al. 1974). This is necessary since PLS-SEM prioritizes the items with respect to their individual reliability. For measurement models to be reliable, the literature suggests composite reliability scores above 0.7 (Nunnally and Bernstein 1994).

Convergent validity assures that all the items correctly measure the same latent variable and are, thus, unidimensional (Henseler et al. 2009). For reflective measurement models in PLS-SEM, convergent validity is assessed based on ensuring that outer loadings (i.e., correlations between variable scores and items) are above 0.708 and that the average variance extracted (AVE) for each variable is above 0.5 (Hair et al. 2014). AVE for a latent variable implies that, on average, more variance in the items is explained by the variable than by measurement errors. Outer loading of an item below 0.708 should be reconsidered since the variation in the item is poorly explained by a variation in the latent variable. If the deletion of an item with outer loadings below 0.708 has positive impacts on AVE and composite reliability, the literature suggests to delete the reflective item from the measurement model (Hair et al. 2011).

Discriminant validity assures that all items are only measuring one variable in the nomological network (Henseler et al. 2009). For measurement models in PLS-SEM, discriminant validity is assured based on checking for *cross-loadings* as well as applying the *Fornell-Larcker criterion*. If an item has a lower correlation with its respective latent variable (i.e., outer loading) than with any other latent variable in the nomological network (i.e., cross-loading), the items or the latent variable should be reconsidered. The Fornell-Larcker criterion compares the square root of each variable's AVE and the variable's correlations with any other variable in the nomological network (Fornell and Larcker 1981). According to the criterion, a variable should share more variance with its corresponding items than with any other variable (Hair et al. 2014). A violation would imply that two variables are empirically not sufficiently different from each other which would imply in turn a lack of *discriminant validity*.

4.2.6 Final Measurement Instrument

The statistical tests introduced were used to ensure that the measurement models are reliable and valid. The presented qualitative and quantitative techniques allowed to ensure that the measurement models exhibit *content, convergent* and *discriminant validity* as well as *indicator* and *composite reliability* (Henseler et al. 2009). At this stage, any items were omitted or refined which had negative impact on the reliability and validity of the measurement instruments. The English version of the final measurement models are presented in Table 4.3. The original German items used in the study are provided in the Appendix in Table B.2.

4.3 Data Collection

Survey data from actual users of cloud storage services was used to explore and understand cloud service relationships. While it is believed that initial adoption is an important step in the relationship between cloud provider and user, the actual relationship does not fully emerge until a cloud user puts his data into the cloud. Therefore, the goal of the study was to evaluate the cloud service relationship theory using a "representative" set of cloud storage service users in Germany (target population). While little is known about which part of the German population is using cloud storage services, a representative set (gender and age) of internet users that matches the general population in Germany was pre-selected and subsequently, those participants of the survey that use the market-leading cloud storage service *Dropbox* were surveyed ensuring comparability of responses.

According to a recent study of the German online research consortium ("Arbeitsgemeinschaft Online Forschung e.V."), 53 % of all German internet users are male and 47 % female. Moreover, internet adopters are younger compared to the entire German population (9.5 % in the ages between 14 and 19, 18.7 % in the ages between 20 and 29, 17.8 % in the ages between 30 and 39, 22.6 % in the ages between 40 and 49, 16.8 % in the ages of 60 or older; cf. AGOF 2013). Fine-grained distribution information from AGOF (incorporating also different gender distributions within age-sets) was used to deduce the requirements on a representative sample of German internet users.

Using these requirements, the professional online panel has sent out individual invitations to its members in the period between 12th of November 2012 and 9th of December 2012. Overall, 4.888 responses were recorded. Two methods were used to estimate the effect of a nonresponse bias on the results as suggested by the literature (Armstrong and Overton 1977). A non-response error biases results if answers of respondents significantly differ from those who did not participate in the survey (Miller and Smith 1983). First, the final sample was compared with known parameters of the population. Since a representative internet user sample with respect to age and gender was collected, the survey covers all important demographic groups (Table 4.4). Second, early and late valid respondents with respect to the days they needed to react on the invitation were compared assuming that respondents who respond less readily are similar to non-respondents (Armstrong and Overton 1977). To compare path estimates and significance levels of early and late respondents the parametric PLS multigroup analyses (PLS-MGA) approach

Table 4.3 Measurement models used in study (english version)

Continuance intention (Bhattacherjee 2001)
CONT1: I intend to continue using Dropbox
CONT2: My intentions are to continue rather than discontinue using Dropbox
CONT3: If I could, I would like to continue my use of Dropbox
CONT4: I plan to discontinue using Dropbox [reverse]

Security concerns (Kim 2008; Pavlou et al. 2007)
SEC1: Dropbox implements security measures to protect my data from outside [reverse]
SEC2: Dropbox usually ensures that transferring information is protected from hacking attacks [reverse]
SEC3: I feel safe in making transactions on Dropbox [reverse]
SEC4: I feel secure in transferring information when using Dropbox [reverse]

Privacy concerns (Kim 2008; Pavlou et al. 2007)
PRIV1: I am concerned that Dropbox will use my personal information for other purposes without my authorization
PRIV2: I am concerned that Dropbox will share my personal information for other purposes without my authorization
PRIV3: I am concerned that Dropbox is collecting too much information about me
PRIV4: I am concerned about my privacy when using Dropbox

Availability concerns (own creation)
AVA1: I am concerned about Dropbox's service availability
AVA2: I am concerned that Dropbox could be temporarily unavailable when I need it
AVA3: I am concerned that Dropbox could be temporarily unaccessible
AVA4: I have doubts as to how reliable Dropbox is in providing high service uptime
AVA5: My data could be temporarily unavailable when stored on Dropbox

Service diagnosticity (Jiang and Benbasat 2007)
DIA1: Dropbox's website is helpful for me to evaluate the service
DIA2: Dropbox's website is helpful in familiarizing me with the service
DIA3: Dropbox's website is helpful for me to understand the performance of the service
DIA4: I expect Dropbox's website to help me get a real feel for how the service operates

Third-party assurances (Gefen 2002)
TPA1: Dropbox has quality certifications from credited institutions
TPA2: Dropbox has impressive credentials
TPA3: There are many reputable third-party certification bodies for assuring the trustworthiness of Dropbox
TPA4: The third-party credentials of Dropbox are impressive

Legal sanctions (D'Arcy et al. 2009; Peace et al. 2003): If Dropbox were caught violating the SLAs,…
LS1: … I think the legal consequences would be very high
LS2: … I think they would be severely punished
LS3: … Dropbox's punishment would be very severe
LS4: … Dropbox would be severely reprimanded

(continued)

Table 4.3 (continued)

Perceived positive WOM influence (Kim and Son 2009)
PWOM1: Others have said positive things about Dropbox to me
PWOM2: People whose I seek for advice have recommended Dropbox to me
PWOM3: My friends have referred me to Dropbox ([a])
PWOM4: My friends and colleagues have encouraged me to use Dropbox

Perceived negative WOM influence (Blodgett et al. 1997)
NWOM1: My friends and relatives have cautioned adainst Dropbox
NWOM2: My friends and relatives have complained about Dropbox
NWOM3: My friends and relatives told me not to use Dropbox
NWOM4: Others have said negative things about Dropbox

Peer adoption (own creation)
PAD1: Many of my friends and colleagues use Dropbox
PAD2: Dropbox is widely distributed among my friends and colleagues
PAD3: If friends and colleagues use a cloud storage service, than most of the time it is Dropbox
PAD4: Dropbox is often used by my friends and colleagues for storing and exchanging data

Knowledge about cloud (own creation)
KNOW1: I understand how cloud technology is functioning
KNOW2: I have a good grasp of how cloud technology works
KNOW3: I can easily recall the functionality provided by cloud technology
KNOW4: It is easy for me to remember how cloud technology functions

Attentiveness to alternatives (Kim and Son 2009)
ATT1: I will try cloud storage services offered by other cloud providers
ATT2: I will try occasionally other cloud storage services
ATT3: I am interested in other cloud storage services
ATT4 I will never try cloud storage services other than Dropbox [reversed]

([a])denotes that item was dropped in main study

was used (Keil et al. 2000b). Apart from one path estimate (H8a: NWOM $\rightarrow$ SEC) which magnitude was higher for late respondents, no significant differences were found between early and late respondents (Table B.8 in appendix). Given the primary interest in identifying potential relationships between variables, one can infer that a non-response error did not affect the conclusions from the study.

Since the goal was to obtain a representative set of respondents, every respondent was initially screened with respect to age and gender. 40 % failed this initial screening process because the quota of their demographic group was already full. Moreover, strong satisficers who were unable to answer the test questions or who were rushing through the survey were removed from the final survey statistic (cf. detailed explanation below). Overall, 2.011 valid responses were obtained which embody a representative sample of German internet users with respect to age and

Table 4.4 Years of age and gender distribution among respondents

Years of age/gender	German internet users		Dropbox users		Difference
	Number	Quota (%)	Number	Quota (%)	Quota (%)
14–19/female	90	4.5	42	6.6	2.1
20–29/female	186	9.2	112	17.6	8.4
30–39/female	170	8.5	36	5.6	−2.9
40–49/female	210	10.4	28	4.4	−6
50–59/female	166	8.3	19	3.0	−5.3
60–69/female	132	6.6	15	2.4	−4.2
14–19/male	95	4.7	54	8.5	3.8
20–29/male	189	9.4	119	18.7	9.3
30–39/male	181	9.0	83	13.0	4
40–49/male	233	11.6	59	9.2	−2.4
50–59/male	180	9.0	40	6.3	−2.7
60–69/male	179	8.9	31	4.9	−4
Overall	2.011	100.0	638	100.0	

gender (Table 4.4). From these valid responses 682 declared to use Dropbox as their main cloud storage service. Dropbox was used because the provider is the market leader for cloud storage services in Germany. From all Dropbox users, attitudes, believes and intentions were measured with respect to their use of the cloud storage service. Apart from the measurement models, various data on how respondents use Dropbox as well as demographic information was collected.

One potential problem in using online survey data is satisficing behavior of respondents (Malhotra 2008). Carefully filling out a survey requires respondents to "interpret the meaning of each question, search their memories extensively for all relevant information, integrate that information carefully into summary judgments, and report those summary judgments in ways that convey their meaning as clearly and precisely as possible" (Krosnick 1991, p. 214). In contrast, *satisficing* describes any behavior of respondents in which they take shortcuts and spend less cognitive effort in completing a survey (Barge and Gehlbach 2012). When respondents are satisficing, "they will be more likely to respond stylistically and their responses will be more susceptible to method bias" (Podsakoff et al. 2012, p. 560). Thus, strong satisficing behavior can have severe consequences on scale reliabilities and variable correlations.

Since online surveys are particularly vulnerable (Barge and Gehlbach 2012), several techniques were deployed to *prevent* and *detect* satisficing behavior. First, a professional online panel was used from which survey respondents were recruited (*satisficing prevention*). The panel recruits panel participants via various email and online marketing campaigns. For participating in the survey, each respondent earned €1.50 which was added to his personal panel account. Once the account of the panel member has reached €20, she or he can redeem a voucher at certain retailers. To prevent misconduct, participants are removed from the panel if they repeatedly engage in satisficing behavior. Retarding the payout and making the payout dependent on long-term good conduct reduces the likelihood that participants engage in satisficing behavior.

Second, an instructional manipulation check (IMC) was used to increase the validity of the data (*satisficing prevention*) (Oppenheimer et al. 2009). On the first page of the survey, several instructions were provided to the respondents needed for completing the survey. In order to determine whether respondents have read these instructions, they were asked to counterintuitively press the 'next' button at the top of the page to get to the next page. Participants who failed this IMC received a warning that the survey tool monitors misconduct and were asked to reread the instructions. Based on two experiments, Oppenheimer et al. (2009) show that such a warning procedure can significantly increase the data quality from respondents who initially fail the IMC. Thus, the IMC is an effective method for satisficing prevention.

Third, a middle response alternative (using 7 point Likert scales) was included as well as any "no opinion" response options were excluded for all items to overall increase data quality (*satisficing prevention*). On the one hand, it is import to include a middle response alternative because a "substantial minority of people do appear to hold attitudinal positions which are genuinely neutral" (Sturgis et al. 2012, p. 21). While there are several explanations why respondents select middle alternatives (e.g., 'hidden don't know', neutral attitude, indeterminate), offering an additional "no-opinion" response does not solve the problem of measurement errors. "No-opinion" responses are at least partly reflections of respondent's perceived task difficulty and motivation (satisficing) rather than reflections of a true lack of opinion which respondent hesitate to disclose (Krosnick et al. 2002). Therefore, recommendations of methodologist were followed as another measure for satisficing prevention and a middle response was included but a "no opinion" response options was excluded from the survey (Sturgis et al. 2012).

Fifth, strong satisfiers were detected using two well-established mechanisms und subsequently deleted. On the one hand, test questions were used to directly detect respondents who did not read questions (*satisficing detection*). Both questions were placed in-between attitudinal questions and were asking respondents to indicate that they have read the questions by checking the middle response of the scale. Respondents who were detected have been removed from the survey. On the other hand, two additional indirect satisficing measures were used to further control for satisficing behavior (*satisficing detection*). Respondents were deleted who exited the survey without finishing ("early termination") and respondents who finished the survey at a speed at which thoughtful answers to each item was impossible ("rushing") (Barge and Gehlbach 2012).

4.4   Results

In the following, descriptive statistics of Dropbox users are introduced. Moreover, using the criteria introduced in Sect. 4.2.5, it is shown that the measurement instruments are reliable and valid. In the third sub-section the results of the structural model evaluation are presented, followed by an exploration of contingency factors in the last sub-section.

4.4.1   Descriptive Statistics of Sample

Table 4.5 depicts the descriptive statistics of surveyed Dropbox users. The statistics highlight that the sample consists of heterogeneous demographic groups of low and highly educated, employed and unemployed, low and high income as well as male and female respondents. This provides evidence that no demographic groups were systematically excluded from the study.

4.4.2   Measurement Instrument Validation

The statistical tests explained in detail in Sect. 4.2.5 were followed to evaluate the measurement models. Internal consistency was checked using composite reliability scores (Table 4.6). All measurement models exhibit satisfactory composite reliability values above 0.7 (Nunnally and Bernstein 1994). All outer loadings were

Table 4.5 Descriptive statistics of dropbox users

Education					
No education	Secondary school	Higher education	Completed vocational training	University degree	Doctorate degree
2 (0.3 %)	129 (20.2 %)	192 (30.1 %)	116 (18.2 %)	195 (30.6 %)	4 (0.6 %)

Occupation				Gender	
In training	Employed	Unemployed or retired	Not specified	Male	Female
221 (34.6 %)	337 (52.8 %)	75 (11.8 %)	5 (0.8 %)	386 (60.5 %)	252 (39.5 %)

Income					
< €500	€501 − €1.500	€1.501 − €2.500	€2.501 − €3.500	> €3.500	Not specified
53 (8.3 %)	128 (20.1 %)	155 (24.3 %)	101 (15.8 %)	97 (15.2 %)	104 (16.3 %)

Age group					
16−19	20−29	30−39	40−49	50−59	60−69
96 (15 %)	231 (36.2 %)	119 (18.7 %)	87 (13.6 %)	59 (9.2 %)	46 (7.2 %)

above the recommended threshold of 0.708 suggesting reliable indicators (see Table B.3 in the appendix for more details on the descriptive statistics and loadings at the item level). At the construct level, convergent validity was assessed based on the AVE (Henseler et al. 2009). All constructs had AVE values above 0.5 suggesting that more than half of the item's variance is explained by the latent variable. Discriminant validity was evaluated based on comparing outer and cross loadings (Table B.3 in the appendix) as well as the Fornell-Larcker criterion (Fornell and Larcker 1981). For each item, the outer loading on its associated latent variable was higher than the cross loadings on all other latent variables. Table 4.6 depicts the square root of each latent variable's AVE in the diagonal. According to Fornell-Larcker criterion, the square root of each latent variable's AVE must be larger than its correlation with any other latent variable (Ringle et al. 2012). Since both criteria are fulfilled, one can conclude that the measurement models exhibit discriminant validity.

Since data for each respondent was obtained using a single measurement method, the recommended procedural and statistical remedies as proposed by Podsakoff et al. (2003) were applied to minimize and control for common method variance (CMV). Respondents' anonymity was protected (among others to minimize social desirability bias), question orders were counterbalanced (among others to minimize priming effects), scales were carefully developed (among others to minimize satisficing), and a psychological separation was ensured between endogenous and exogenous variables (among others to minimize consistency bias).

Apart from the procedural remedies, three statistical tests were used to control for CMV. First, the Harman's single factor test was conducted using an exploratory factor analysis in SPSS (Podsakoff et al. 2003). The unrotated principal component factor analysis revealed ten factors with eigenvalues above 1, explaining 82 % of the variance. The most prominent component accounted for 29 % of the variance. Since neither a single factor emerged, nor one general factor accounts for the majority of the covariance among the variables, evidence is provided that CMV did not bias the results (Malhotra et al. 2006).

Second, the marker-variable technique as proposed by Lindell and Whitney (2001) was used to examine how a potential CMV biases the results. The marker-variable technique controls for CMV by including "a measure of the assumed source of method variance as a covariate in the statistical analysis" (Podsakoff et al. 2003, p. 889). The technique was used in a post-hoc manner by taking the second smallest correlation among the variables to be the extent of CMV (0.002 between LS ↔ PWOM as well as LS ↔ NWOM, cf. Table 4.6). The CMV-adjusted estimate and the test statistic for each pair of the correlation matrix were calculated (using equations (4) and (5) in Lindell and Whitney 2001, p. 116). Because the CMV-estimate (second smallest correlation) was close to zero, all previously significant correlations remained significant (Table 4.7). Thus, the marker-variable technique also suggests that CMV did not bias the results.

Third, the latent variables and measures were reconstructed in AMOS 22 to include a latent general common method factor that was allowed to load on every item in the research model (Podsakoff et al. 2003). Since the common variance

Table 4.6 Measurement model validation

VAR	CR	1	2	3	4	5	6	7	8	9	10
1.CONT	0.94	**0.891**									
2.SEC	0.95	-0.372**	**0.906**								
3.PRIV	0.96	-0.278**	0.538**	**0.933**							
4.AVA	0.94	-0.183**	0.354**	0.541**	**0.866**						
5.DIA	0.95	0.279**	-0.508**	-0.268**	-0.121**	**0.914**					
6.TPA	0.98	0.262**	-0.513**	-0.298**	-0.143**	0.436**	**0.953**				
7.LS	0.96	0.159**	-0.347**	-0.199**	-0.055	0.377**	0.377**	**0.917**			
8.PWOM	0.88	0.275**	-0.263**	-0.193**	-0.119**	0.203**	0.332**	0.002	**0.839**		
9.NWOM	0.92	-0.309**	0.188**	0.305**	0.283**	-0.156**	-0.087*	-0.049	0.002	**0.864**	
10.PAD	0.95	0.323**	-0.224**	-0.144**	-0.124**	0.269**	0.360**	0.119*	0.542**	-0.026	**0.915**

Note The (bold) diagonal elements represent AVE
* denotes significant correlations at $p < 0.05$
** denotes significant correlations at $p < 0.01$

Table 4.7 CMV-adjusted correlation matrix

VAR	1	2	3	4	5	6	7	8	9
1.CONT									
2.SEC	−0.375**								
3.PRIV	−0.281**	0.537**							
4.AVA	−0.185**	0.353**	0.540**						
5.DIA	0.278**	−0.511**	−0.271**	−0.123**					
6.TPA	0.261**	−0.516**	−0.301**	−0.145**	0.435**				
7.LS	0.157*	−0.350**	−0.201**	−0.057	0.376**	0.376**			
8.PWOM	0.274**	−0.266**	−0.195**	−0.121**	0.201**	0.331**	0.000		
9.NWOM	−0.312**	0.186**	0.304**	0.282**	−0.158**	−0.089*	−0.051	0.000	
10.PAD	0.322**	−0.226**	−0.146**	−0.126**	0.268**	0.359**	0.117*	0.541**	−0.028

* denotes significant correlations at $p < 0.05$
** denotes significant correlations at $p < 0.01$

between the measures and the latent general common method factor was also close to zero, it can be concluded that the path estimates and significance levels are neither inflated nor deflated by CMV (MacKenzie et al. 1999). Overall, based on these three statistical tests, any concern that a CMV biases the results can be ruled out.

4.4.3 Structural Model Evaluation

Once evidence is provided that the measurement model is both reliable and valid, the next step is to evaluate the structural model. For evaluating the structural model, multicollinearity, path estimates and significance levels as well as mediating effects were assessed (Hair et al. 2014).

As the PLS algorithm assumes that there is no collinearity between the exogenous latent variables, one needs to ensure that this is the case for each endogenous latent variable. Using the latent variables scores of each variable, a linear regression was run using SPSS and the variance inflation factor (VIF) was calculated based on the regression (Mooi and Sarstedt 2011). The VIF measures how much of the variance of an estimated regression coefficient is increased because of collinearity, i.e., because two exogenous latent variables are correlated. The VIF for all correlations was far below the recommended threshold of 5 (even all VIF were below 2) suggesting that multicollinearity did not bias path coefficient estimations.

Subsequently, the PLS-algorithm was used to estimate path coefficients. Moreover, significance levels were estimated based on the bootstrapping algorithm with 5.000 subsamples. Overall, mixed results are obtained regarding the structural model (Table 4.8).

While data-related concerns significantly influence continuance intention (H1a: $\beta = -0.312$, $p < 0.01$; H1b: $\beta = -0.1$, $p < 0.05$), dependency-related concerns (availability) have no significant influence (H1c: $\beta = -0.018$; $p > 0.1$). Apart from availability evaluations (H4c: $\beta = -0.027$, $p > 0.1$; H5c: $\beta = -0.076$; $p < 0.1$), signaling mechanisms (service diagnosticity and third-party assurances) have strong and significant influence on cloud users' evaluation of the service (H4a: $\beta = -0.307$, $p < 0.01$; H4b: $\beta = -0.112$, $p < 0.01$; H5a: $\beta = -0,310$, $p < 0.01$; H5b: $\beta = -0.17$, $p < 0.01$). In turn, incentives have just a mixed influence on cloud users' evaluation of the service. While security concerns are significantly reduced (H6a: $\beta = -0.098$, $p < 0.01$), privacy and availability evaluations are not significantly affected (H6b: $\beta = -0.066$, $p < 0.1$; H6c: $\beta = 0.009$, $p > 0.1$).

Mixed results are also obtained for social influence processes. The empirical results suggest that internalization-based processes are important for users' evaluation of the cloud service (H7a: $\beta = -0.1$, $p < 0.01$; H7b: $\beta = -0.114$, $p < 0.01$; H7c: $\beta = -0.077$, $p < 0.1$). Interestingly, negative WOM had a stronger effect on cloud users' evaluations than positive opinions about the service among peers (H8a: $\beta = 0.108$, $p < 0.01$; H8b: $\beta = 0.267$, $p < 0.01$, H8c: $\beta = 0.269$, $p < 0.01$). In contrast to internalization, identification-based processes did not significantly affect the

Table 4.8 Structural model evaluation

Proposition	Hypothesis	Path coefficient	t values	p	Interpretation
Adverse selection	H1a: SEC → CONT	−0.312	6.4856	<0.01	Supported
Moral hazard	H1b: PRIV → CONT	−0.100	1.9131	<0.05	Supported
Adverse selection	H1c: AVA → CONT	−0.018	0.3812	>0.10	Not supported
Signals	H4a: DIA → SEC	−0.307	7.4344	<0.01	Supported
Signals	H4b: DIA → PRIV	−0.112	2.3094	<0.01	Supported
Signals	H4c: DIA → AVA	−0.027	0.5378	>0.10	Not supported
Signals	H5a: TPA → SEC	−0.310	7.0410	<0.01	Supported
Signals	H5b: TPA → PRIV	−0.170	3.6671	<0.01	Supported
Signals	H5c: TPA → AVA	−0.076	1.5657	<0.10	Not supported
Incentives	H6a: LS → SEC	−0.098	2.4694	<0.01	Supported
Incentives	H6b: LS → PRIV	−0.066	1.5037	<0.10	Not supported
Incentives	H6c: LS → AVA	0.009	0.1932	>0.10	Not supported
Internalization	H7a: PWOM → SEC	−0.100	2.5824	<0.01	Supported
Internalization	H7b: PWOM → PRIV	−0.114	2.6317	<0.01	Supported
Internalization	H7c: PWOM → AVA	−0.077	1.6094	<0.10	Not supported
Internalization	H8a: NWOM → SEC	0.108	3.1909	<0.01	Supported
Internalization	H8b: NWOM → PRIV	0.267	7.4652	<0.01	Supported
Internalization	H8c: NWOM → AVA	0.269	7.0417	<0.01	Supported
Identification	H9a: PAD → SEC	0.035	0.9029	>0.10	Not supported
Identification	H9b: PAD → PRIV	0.022	0.5120	>0.10	Not supported
Identification	H9c: PAD → AVA	−0.035	0.7883	>0.10	Not supported

evaluation of the cloud service (H9a: $\beta = 0.0351$, $p > 0.1$; H9b: $\beta = 0.022$, $p > 0.1$; H9c: $\beta = -0.035$, $p > 0.1$).

Given that the goal of the study was to explore relationships rather than maximizing the explained variance, a considerable amount of the variance of cloud users' continuance intention (R^2[CONT] = 0.15) as well as the evaluation of the cloud service (R^2[SEC] = 0.39, R^2[PRIV] = 0.2, R^2[AVA] = 0.1) is explained. The effect sizes of the social influence processes are small for security concerns

(f^2[SEC] = 0,02) and medium for privacy and availability (f^2[PRIV] = 0.11, f^2[AVA] = 0.11) (Cohen 1988).

In order to evaluate the role of bounded rationality, the PLS-MGA approach was chosen (Keil et al. 2000b). Using a median split, the user sample was divided into groups of users with high (n = 319) versus low (n = 319) knowledge about cloud as well as into groups of users with high (n = 318) versus low (n = 320) interest in alternative cloud service (Table 4.9). In order to check whether parameter estimates differ significantly between groups, the Levene's inferential test statistic was used which evaluates if the obtained differences in sample variances have occurred based on random sampling from a population with equal variances or not (Mooi and Sarstedt 2011). Both group comparisons provide consistent results suggesting that bounded rationality applies to moral hazard (H2b: |p(high knowledge) − p(low knowledge)| = 0.175, p < 0.05; H3b: |p(high interest) − p(low interest)| = 0.189, p < 0.05) but not to adverse selection problems (H2a: |p(high knowledge) − p(low knowledge)| = 0.054, p > 0.1; H2c: |p(high knowledge) − p(low knowledge)| = 0.025, H3a: p > 0.1; H3a: |p(high knowledge) − p(low knowledge)| = 0.127, p > 0.05); H3c: |p(high knowledge) − p(low knowledge)| = 0.028, p > 0.1).

The research model implicitly includes several mediating effects. The approach by Zhao et al. (2010) was used to test these mediating effects. Using the bootstrapping procedure as a stronger alternative to the common Sobel test (Preacher and Hayes 2004), almost all significant mediating paths were assessed as complementary mediations (Table 4.10). A complementary mediation describes a situation in which both a mediated and direct effect exists pointing at the same direction (Zhao et al. 2010). Only NWOM → PRIV → CONT turned out to be a non-mediating path for the full sample. However, using the two sub samples—high cloud knowledge as well as high interest in alternatives (Table 4.9)—this mediating relationship was also identified as complementary. A complementary mediation provides evidence for the hypothesized mediator but also provides cue for an omitted mediator in the direct path. As only cloud-specific concerns were considered as sources of cloud users' uncertainty, the results of the mediation analysis provide support for the cloud service relationship theory.

4.4.4 Contingency Factor Evaluation

So far the structural model evaluation has assumed that the sample consists of homogenous observations. However, if different path estimates are present for different sub groups of the sample (called heterogeneity of observations), this can have severe consequences for the validity of the PLS-SEM results (Hair et al. 2014). Although the heterogeneity of observations can never be fully known a priori, researchers are advised to collect additional data that can characterize different types of cloud service users (Hair et al. 2011).

Both demographic and user type information were collected to form groups of observations and compare them with respect to path estimates and significance

Table 4.9 PLS-SEM multigroup analysis (bounded rationality)

Proposition	Hypothesis	Group 1: High knowledge (n = 319)			Group 3: High interest (n = 318)		
		p(1)	se(p(1))	t(1)	p(3)	se(p(3))	t(3)
	SEC → CONT	−0.267	0.0547	4.8829	−0.247	0.0394	6.2805
	PRIV → CONT	−0.190	0.0497	3.8207	−0.179	0.0472	3.7972
	AVA → CONT	−0.037	0.0505	0.7371	−0.027	0.0447	0.6133
	Hypothesis	Group 2: Low knowledge (n = 319)			Group 4: Low interest (n = 320)		
		p(2)	se(p(2))	t(2)	p(4)	se(p(4))	t(4)
	SEC → CONT	−0.321	0.0420	7.6328	−0.374	0.0582	6.4293
	PRIV → CONT	−0.015	0.0544	0.2737	0.010	0.0611	0.1705
	AVA → CONT	−0.012	0.0464	0.2482	0.001	0.0521	0.0100
		Group 1 versus Group 2			Group 3 versus Group 4		
		|p(1)−p(2)|	t(1−2)	p	|p(3)−p(4)|	t(3−4)	p
Bounded Rationality	H2/3a: SEC → CONT	0.054	0.7842	0.433 (not supported)	0.127	1.8097	0.071 (not supported)
	H2/3b: PRIV → CONT	0.175	2.3787	0.018 (supported)	0.189	2.4515	0.015 (supported)
	H2/3c: AVA → CONT	0.025	0.3651	0.715 (not supported)	0.028	0.4085	0.683 (not supported)

Table 4.10 Mediator analysis for significant paths (all Dropbox users)

Independent variable	Mediator (M)	Dependent variable	Is indirect effect significant?	Is direct effect significant?	Is effect consistent?	Type of mediation (Zhao et al. 2010)
Service diagnosticity	Security concerns	Continuance intention	Yes/Yes	Yes	Yes	*Complementary*
Third-party assurance	Security concerns	Continuance intention	Yes/Yes	Yes	Yes	*Complementary*
Legal sanctions	Security concerns	Continuance intention	Yes/Yes	No		*Full mediation*
Positive WOM	Security concerns	Continuance intention	Yes/Yes	Yes	Yes	*Complementary*
Negative WOM	Security concerns	Continuance intention	Yes/Yes	Yes	Yes	*Complementary*
Service Diagnosticity	Privacy concerns	Continuance intention	Yes/Yes	Yes	Yes	*Complementary*
Third-party assurance	Privacy concerns	Continuance intention	Yes/Yes	Yes	Yes	*Complementary*
Positive WOM	Privacy concerns	Continuance intention	Yes/Yes	Yes	Yes	*Complementary*
Negative WOM	Privacy concerns	Continuance intention	Yes/No	Yes		*Direct-only*

levels. Four contingency factors were used to create sub samples from the data (Table 4.11 for details on the operationalization of the contingency factors). On the one hand, demographic information regarding respondents' age and gender were used to split the sample in female and male groups as well as young and old cloud users (using a median split). On the other hand, user type information was exploited to form sub groups of the sample. First, respondents were asked to self-assess whether they store sensitive data in Dropbox. Second, respondents had to report the degree to which business data from their job is stored in the cloud.

In order to explore whether the cloud service relationship theory provides consistent results across different user settings, four multi-group analyses were conducted using PLS-MGA (Keil et al. 2000b). The detailed results can be found in the appendix. Three types of significant structural differences were distinguished among sub groups: (1) Magnitude differences refer to statistically significant differences among groups with respect to the magnitude of significant path estimates. (2) Sign differences refer to statistically significant differences between groups with respect to the sign of significant path estimates. (3) Significance level differences refer to statistically significant differences between groups with respect to the significant level of the relationship. Overall, the four group comparisons (which entailed 84 path estimate and significance level comparisons) identified in total five magnitude differences, one sign difference and nine significance level differences (Tables B.4, B.5, B.6 and B.7 in the appendix). Since four differences between groups are statistically expected (number of comparisons × (1 − confidence interval)), it can be concluded that heterogeneity of observations does not impact the validity of the structural model evaluation.

Table 4.11 Operationalization of contingency factors

Item	Group 1: Highly sensitive data		Group 2: Less sensitive data	
	Mean	Std	Mean	Std
If my data would be published, that would be... ... a big problem (0) ... no problem (100)	7.71	9.73	55.75	28.57
Critical (0) ... not critical (100)	7.60	8.73	53.93	28.39
Disastrous (0) ... whatever! (100)	13.23	13.61	61.02	22.93
	Group 3: Only private use		Group 4: Business and private use	
	Mean	Std	Mean Std	
What percentage of your data do you use for professional purposes? (in per cent)	2.73	1.86	37.60	29.37
	Group 5: Young		Group 6: Old	
	Mean	Std	Mean	Std
How old are you? (in ages)	22.08	3.58	45.33	10.21
	Group 7: Female		Group 8: Male	
What is your gender?	Female (N = 252)		Male (N = 386)	

4.5 Discussion

The effort that was taken in the scale development process and the remedies deployed for preventing and detecting satisficing behavior were worthwhile. Only one item had to be dropped due to lower outer loadings on the latent variable. Internal consistency reliability, indicator reliability, convergent as well as discriminant validity was confirmed by several empirical tests for the final measurement instrument (Hair et al. 2014). Overall, it can be concluded that reliable and valid measurement instruments were used. Further, recommended procedural and statistical remedies were applied to prevent and control for CMV. Based on three recommended statistical tests (Podsakoff et al. 2003), it can be concluded that CMV did not bias the path estimates and significance levels.

Overall, very interesting results were obtained from the empirical evaluation. These results are discussed in the following. First, key findings from the study are interpreted. Subsequently, the contribution to IS theory is carved out. Lastly, the limitations of the empirical evaluation are discussed.

4.5.1 Key Findings

Mixed but somehow consistent results were obtained from path estimations and significance tests. Security concerns have been shown to be the strongest source of uncertainty in cloud service relationships. The concept has been frequently used for understanding e–commerce purchase intensions (Pavlou et al. 2007; Salisbury et al. 2001) or the awareness of web assurance seals (Kim et al. 2008). Yet, to the knowledge of the author this study is the first to integrate security concerns into the nomological network of IT service user behavior. Privacy concerns have been identified as the second strongest source of uncertainty in cloud service relationships. The concept of privacy concerns has been well-established in IS research. As this study, privacy research studies seek to explain levels of privacy concerns and aim to explore the effects of privacy concerns on various dependent variables (Belanger and Crossler 2011; Smith et al. 2011) using various theoretical lenses (Li 2012). Similar to security concerns, a majority of research examines how privacy affects individual's intention to participate in e-commerce transactions (Belanger et al. 2002). The cloud service relationship context differs from e-commerce scenarios with respect to the good or service traded over the internet. While e-commerce research differentiates between trading search goods (Pavlou et al. 2007) and experience goods (Dimoka et al. 2012) over an e-commerce platform, cloud services are best described as credence goods, i.e., it is impossible for the user to fully evaluate the qualities and actions of the provider even after the adoption has taken place. Given that cloud users transfer rich, sensitive and personal data to the cloud provider, individual's ongoing acceptance of a cloud service is considerable different to scenarios examined in the stream of "information privacy and e-business impacts" (Belanger and Crossler 2011, p. 1020). Therefore, reexamining privacy and security concerns in the context of individual's acceptance of cloud services is an important endeavor.

In the context of cloud storage services, availability concerns represent no significant source of uncertainty for the cloud service relationship. This finding is also consistent across almost all sub samples that were explored through the contingency factor analysis. Only for older cloud users, availability concerns are incorporated into the evaluation of the cloud service. Because of the particularities of the study context, the role of availability concerns should be reexamined for other cloud service relationships. Dropbox offers a synchronization function which enables users to edit and re-post files from different devices without overwriting versions. Therefore, a temporary outage of the service has only minor consequences for users compared to other widely-adopted cloud services such as cloud-based customer relationship services (Benlian et al. 2011) where business processes are fully dependent on a reliable uptime of the cloud service and where outages of the service have severe consequences. Therefore, future researchers are encouraged to reexamine the cloud service relationship theory in scenarios where high availability is an even more important requirement.

Apart from the instantiations of agency problems, interesting results were obtained from the examination of bounded rationality. On the one hand, no differences were identified among the subsamples with respect to the influence of security and availability concerns (adverse selection problems) on continuance. Regardless of the knowledge about and interest in cloud services, all groups equally incorporate quality concerns into the behavioral intention. On the other hand, significant differences were identified among the sub samples with respect to the influence of privacy concerns on continuance intention. Cloud users with low knowledge about or low interest in alternative cloud services may have privacy concerns but do not incorporate this in their choice of the "right" cloud service. Rather, they have a lower aspiration level on a satisfactory cloud service alternative which includes a calculus that their personal data is used for secondary purposes or disclosed to third parties without their consent (Kim 2008). Thus first empirical evidence and an explanation for the 'privacy paradox' is provided that has yet not been linked to IT service user behavior (Acquisti 2004). Cloud users with low knowledge about and interest in alternative cloud services tend to discount the risks of information disclosure because potential negative consequences take place in the distant future while the benefits of using the cloud service happen today (O'Donoghue and Rabin 2001). In contrast, cloud users with high knowledge about and interest in alternative cloud services have a higher aspiration level on a satisfactory cloud service with respect to the anticipated actions of the cloud provider. These findings also provide strong practical implications for IT managers who are planning to advocate the controlled uptake of cloud services within their organization (Harris et al. 2012). In order to fully incorporate negative consequences of information disclosure, cloud users need sufficient cloud knowledge as well as attentiveness to alternatives to ensure that adoption processes are aligned with enterprise's IT governance objectives.

Beyond a better understanding of the interaction between uncertainty evaluations and behavioral intentions, insights were also obtained about the role of different safeguarding mechanisms that mitigate cloud users' uncertainty perceptions. Service diagnosticity—a concept derived from the e-commerce literature—was shown to mitigate the evaluation process of users in cloud service relationship. While availability concerns are not affected, security and privacy concerns can significantly be mitigated by this quality-signaling mechanism. Besides first-party information that is directly provided by the cloud provider, third-party mechanisms provide independent verification of a cloud provider's quality (Özpolat et al. 2013). Just like service diagnosticity, third-party assurances significantly reduce cloud users' uncertainty. Overall, the results highlight the importance of signaling-mechanisms for reducing information asymmetries in cloud service relationships (Akerlof 1970).

Compared to signals, the results show that legal sanctions play a minor role for mitigating uncertainties in cloud service relationships. Only security concerns are significantly affected by users' perception that cloud providers are sanctioned if they violate SLAs. A possible explanation of this finding is that cloud users have a higher certainty that security breaches get uncovered compared to violations with respect to secondary use or disclosure of cloud users' data. Overall, it can carefully be concluded that for cloud services whose performance is hard to evaluate legal sanctions cannot fully align the interest of cloud provider and cloud users and thus cannot reduce agency costs.

Apart from bilateral governance mechanisms, the study shows that internalization-based social influence processes strongly shape cloud users' evaluation of the cloud service. Previous research has primarily studied why users engage in WOM activities offline (Anderson 1998) as well as online (Hennig-Thurau et al. 2004) and the effect of WOM on purchasing decision-making. However, the role of WOM as a special form of social influence has not been linked to IT service user behavior. The results suggest two things. First, WOM of either valence influences the evaluation of cloud services. Thereby, it is important to note that internalization processes are different from online feedback mechanisms. Online feedback mechanisms can be used by providers as signaling mechanisms where virtual strangers are assuring the quality of the service. However, while second-party online-feedback mechanisms are useful for reducing product uncertainty in e-commerce scenarios (Dimoka et al. 2012; Pavlou and Gefen 2004), the study highlights that cloud users put special emphasis on opinions of their social peers in their evaluation of the cloud service rather than virtual strangers. Second, negative opinions (e.g., in the form of word of warning) have stronger influence than positive opinions (e.g., in the form of service recommendations). This corroborates earlier research indicating that receivers of WOM place different weight on these influence processes in making evaluations (Richins 1983).

While internalization was shown to be an important social influence process, identification-based social influence processes did hardly affect cloud users' evaluation of the service. A possible explanation is that the role of identification-based social influence processes decreases with the accumulation of service experience (Thompson et al. 1991), while the effects of internalization persist over longer time periods (Wang et al. 2013). With growing experience cloud users more strongly focus on their own judgment or concrete reference opinions about the qualities and actions of the cloud provider (Venkatesh and Morris 2000), rather than the behavior of relevant peers. Future research should re-examine the role of peer adoption for less experienced cloud users (e.g., nonusers).

4.5.2 Theoretical Contributions

The development and evaluation of the cloud service relationship contributes to the IT innovation and adoption theory in different ways.

As highlighted earlier, cloud services are different from the traditional technologies that have been in focus of IT adoption research. Research on IT user behavior has examined functional (e.g., performance and effort expectancy, Venkatesh et al. 2003), organizational (e.g., top management support, user support, social norms, Jeyaraj et al. 2006) or more recently motivational (e.g., perceived locus of causality,

Malhotra et al. 2008) factors that influence individual's evaluation and utilization of IT (Fichman 2004). In contrast to IT product scenarios where IT users are relatively independent from the IT provider once they have deployed the software, cloud users depend on the cloud provider over the whole life-cycle of cloud service utilization and have only limited information about the cloud provider's qualities and actions. This important new aspect has been focus of this study.

Advancing principal-agent theory using complementing theories (Eisenhardt 1989a), this study contributes to IS theory by developing and empirically validating a theory that explains how uncertainties arise and how they can be mitigated in ongoing cloud service relationships. First, sources of uncertainty are disentangled in cloud service relationships and linked to the nomological network of IT user behavior. Second, the study refines the understanding of the role of bounded rationality in cloud service relationships by characterizing users who differently take uncertainty evaluation under consideration in their decision-making. Third, the study sheds light on the role of different safeguarding mechanisms in cloud service relationships. On the one hand, it confirms the important role of signals for reducing information asymmetries in online exchange environments. While quality signaling mechanisms are very important (Dimoka et al. 2012; Özpolat et al. 2013), incentives only play a marginal role in cloud service relationships. On the other hand, the study reveals that while internalization-based social influence processes have a persistent role for the cloud user's evaluation of the service, the role of identification-based processes seems to diminish with the accumulation of service experience. This finding is in line with prior work on the effects of social influence processes on IT user behavior that has highlighted changing susceptibility of users regarding social influence processes (e.g., Venkatesh and Morris 2000).

Overall, the study contributes to cloud research by investigating the effects of agency problems and safeguarding mechanisms on the intention to continue using a cloud service. This work enables future research on cloud service relationships as it is outlined in the follow-up chapter.

4.5.3 Implications for Practice

The findings can be used by governments, IT departments and IT providers as a sensitive device for understanding cloud service relationships and for developing their cloud service strategies. A summary of the most important managerial implications is provided in Table 4.12. The latter in brackets stands for the respective stakeholder for whom the managerial implication is relevant. The discussion about the implications is structured along the safeguarding mechanisms identified that mitigate uncertainties in cloud service relationships.

Since the study highlights the important role of quality signaling mechanisms (service diagnosticity and third-party assurance), IT providers should offer a clear and transparent website and should deploy online feedback mechanisms allowing cloud users to learn from other users—most often virtual strangers—about the high

Table 4.12 Implications for practice

Mechanisms	Managerial implications
Service diagnosticity	• Provide a clear and transparent website (P)
	• Allow users to provide feedback (P)
Third-party assurances	• Use credible and differently costly seals and make them visible to the user (P)
	• Ensure that accreditation institutions for cloud services are available for cloud providers (G)
Legal sanctions	• Declare to sanction violations against the SLAs (P)
	• Provide legal framework, e.g., for privacy violations (G)
Positive WOM	• Offer simple and visible tools to customers to minimize their effort to spread positive word about the service (P)
	• Allow users to invite peers to adopt cloud service (P)
	• Make use of opinion leaders promoting adoption (D)
Negative WOM	• Get active when negative WOM activities take place in users' social networks (P)
	• Offer direct feedback mechanisms that allow users to bilaterally provide negative feedback (P)
Peer Adoption	• Offer low entrance barriers for users who are exposed to WOM and want to invite peers (P)
Bounded rationality	• Educate users and provide a transparent cloud market (D,G)

Letter in brackets indicates for whom (*D* IT department, *G* government, *P* provider) managerial implication is relevant

quality of the service. Moreover, quality seals from reputable institutions should be made clearly visible to users. To facilitate a transparent market, government authorities should ensure that accreditation authorities are available.

Although legal sanctions only marginally influence uncertainty evaluations, cloud provider should nevertheless see SLAs as a mechanism for aligning their interests with users and thereby mitigating uncertainties. Further, government authorities should provide a legal framework that allows users to sue providers for compensation if SLAs are violated. This would make SLAs a more effective measure to reduce uncertainties.

Beyond bilateral mechanisms, the study highlights the possibility to utilize social contagion effects fostering the diffusion and adoption of cloud services among social peers (positive and negative WOM). Therefore, cloud provider should offer simple and visible tools to customers to minimize their effort to spread positive word about the service and invite friends and colleagues to adopt the service. Also IT departments should utilize opinion leaders to promote the software adoption within the organization. Further the study highlight the importance of getting active when negative WOM activities take place in users' social networks. Users spend more and more time on social networking sites and less on provider websites. Therefore, providers should monitor sentiments in social networks with respect to their services and should get active if negative WOM activities take place. They also should offer simple and direct feedback mechanisms that allow users to bilaterally provide negative feedback without social contagion effects and the possibility to directly react on complaints of discontented customers.

Finally, IT departments should be aware that knowledge about and interest in alternatives are important requirements allowing cloud users to fully incorporate uncertainty evaluation in their behavior. Therefore, they should educate user and provide information about cloud service alternatives. Also government authorities should protect users from disclosing their private data to low quality cloud services by increasing the transparency of the cloud service market.

4.5.4 Limitations

A few limitations of the empirical evaluation have to be mentioned. First, a representative sample of panel participants was used for testing the cloud service relationship theory. There exists some evidence that panel participants are different to the rest of the population: e.g., panelists tend to be earlier adopters of technology than other survey respondents (Duffy et al. 2005). Moreover, panel conditioning which occurs when panel participants get more experienced with filling out surveys represents another problem. Given their experiences, responses from panelist may differ from the responses of the rest of the population (Göritz 2007). Future research should recruit respondents which are not members of an online panel to corroborate the findings.

Apart from the recruiting process, several measures were used to carefully detect and delete strong satisficers. While measures were employed to prevent respondents from satsficing behavior and only a very conservative deletion approach was chosen (Barge and Gehlbach 2012), a possible bias has to be mentioned. Since no data exist to evaluate whether satisficers are systematically different to non-satisficers, an estimate whether the path estimates are biased by the elimination of satisficers cannot be provided. Anecdotal evidence that satisficers and non-satisficers are not systematically different is provided by Oppenheimer et al. (2009) who disciplined non-diligent respondents and did not find any systematic differences.

Third, cloud storage services were used as a study context for the evaluation. Cloud storage services are widely adopted by internet users and exhibit the typical characteristics of cloud services. The results suggest that the sources of uncertainty might be dependent on specific sub-characteristics of the cloud service. Availability concerns may represent a stronger source of uncertainties in scenarios where business processes fully depend on the cloud service (e.g., customer relationship cloud services: Benlian et al. 2009). Therefore, future research should reexamine the role of availability concerns as a source of uncertainty in cloud service relationships.

4.6 Summary

The goal of this chapter was to empirically evaluate and refine the cloud service relationship theory in the emerging context of cloud storage services. This chapter provided a clear and transparent record on how the empirical study was conducted. A comprehensive scale development study was introduced that was very valuable for developing reliable and valid measurement instruments. Further, the sampling strategy and how the survey was administered were presented. Results of both measurement model and structural model evaluation were introduced in detail. Lastly, the findings were discussed in the light of the extant knowledge about IS and the theoretical contribution of the study was carved out. Finally, implications for practice and limitations of the study were presented.

Chapter 5
Summary and Outlook

*Why should IS researchers have any concern for individual IS?
Perhaps we might begin with the recognition that we are fairly
benighted about the phenomena. We might also recognize that
these systems represent the most recent frontier for the design of
computer based IS. These are complicated and unique systems
that cross the boundaries between work and home. [...] The list
of possible research questions seems endless. Individual IS may
well be an extremely large, undiscovered, arena for future IS
research.*

Richard Baskerville (2011) in the European Journal of
Information Systems

Abstract This chapter summarizes how this dissertation has addressed the research questions and gives an outlook on future cloud research. First, an overview over identified research practices in the emerging field of positivist cloud research is given and the potential of these practices to advance theorizing about emerging IT innovations is explained. Second, it is highlighted how the developed research framework was applied in the cloud service relationship theory development process. Third, the empirical evaluation of the theory is reflected and key insights are presented. Finally, avenues for future research are identified that can build upon the foundation laid by this work.

5.1 Developing a Framework for Theorizing About IT Innovations

IS research is characterized by temporary burst of interest in emerging IT innovations (Baskerville and Myers 2009). Just like office automation in the 1980s, business process reengineering in the 1990s, and e-commerce in the 2000s, currently a collective belief in IS research and practice exists that cloud technology leads to rational IT innovation (Armbrust et al. 2010). While cloud services are built on many well-established technical concepts, the cloud seems to have the right

© Springer International Publishing Switzerland 2015   75
J. Huntgeburth, *Developing and Evaluating a Cloud Service Relationship Theory*,
Progress in IS, DOI 10.1007/978-3-319-10280-1_5

momentum to shaken the IT industry as a whole. For IS researchers to jump on the cloud bandwagon, the core question is: which socio-technical phenomena surrounding cloud computing are actually new and which phenomena can already be sufficiently explained by the IS knowledge base (Huntgeburth et al. 2012).

While IS research provides good standards to evaluate what constitutes a theoretical contribution (Bacharach 1989; Gregor 2006; Whetten 1989), only little guidance on the process of theorizing is provided. This was the first research gap this dissertation aimed to address. I therefore decided to learn from and reflect upon current cloud research practices to develop a research framework for theorizing about emerging IT innovations. A structured literature review of the IS knowledge base was conducted where articles examining cloud-related socio-technical phenomena were searched. Based on a comprehensive literature analysis process, five distinct categories of heuristics used for theorizing about emerging cloud innovations were identified: "Instantiation", "Laundry-List", "Making an Assumption", "Making an Analogy", and "Challenge the Obvious". Besides identifying these common research practices, the heuristics were also evaluated based on their potential for producing scientific progress. According to the falsificationists' account of science (our evaluation framework), scientific progress consists primarily in the confirmation of bold conjectures and the rejection of central theories and assumptions of the research paradigm (Kuhn 1962).

The "Instantiation" heuristic produces new insights by adapting and testing an existing IS research model in a new empirical setting, whereas the "Laundry-List" describes a heuristic for theorizing, in which a research model (or a laundry list of factors) is almost arbitrary developed in absence of a coherent theoretical perspective. Both heuristics essentially use the existent knowledge about IS and re-test this knowledge in the new empirical context. The potential of these heuristics to create new insights is thus very limited. "Making an Assumption" and "Making an Analogy" have the potential to advance the knowledge about IS because they take the characteristics of the IT innovation into account and may provide new perspectives on the emerging IT innovation phenomena. "Making an Assumption" describes a heuristic for theorizing assuming that a new aspect plays a significant role in the emerging IT innovation context and elaborate on this aspect in detail, whereas "Making an Analogy" provides new insights on a phenomenon by assuming that the socio-technical phenomenon surrounding the IT innovation is similar to something examined in a different research area. The theoretical knowledge about this related phenomenon is subsequently utilized for theorizing. Lastly, the "Challenge the Obvious" heuristic puts well-established knowledge about IS into question by showing that in some cloud-specific situations the extant knowledge about IS does not sufficiently explain behavior or success. Overall, five theory-building practices were identified entailing different potentials for advancing theorizing about emerging IT innovations.

5.2 Developing a Cloud Service Relationship Theory

The second part of the dissertation has built on the research framework and has developed a theory that explains how uncertainties arise in cloud service relationships and how they can be mitigated. Cloud services empower users to design their own IT infrastructure, thereby blurring the boundaries between private and enterprise IT (Harris et al. 2012; Huntgeburth et al. 2013b). Therefore, cloud service relationships become more and more ubiquitous. Cloud service relationships describe bilateral economic exchange situations between cloud users and cloud providers based on standardized SLAs. The cloud provider offers a cloud user highly standardized software services hosted on a shared public infrastructure accessible over the internet. Thereby, the cloud user transfers his personal or business data to the cloud provider.

The cloud service relationship theory development utilized the research framework for theorizing about emerging IT innovations (Table 5.1). As a first logical step, *the assumption was made* that uncertainty is an important aspect for explaining user behavior in cloud service relationships. The shift from IT-as-a-product to IT-as-a-service implies that the user depends on the provider at all times and has only limited information about the provider's qualities, intentions, and actions. This aspect has been widely neglected in previous research on individual IT user behavior and therefore warranted an examination in the emerging context of cloud service relationships.

Second, because goal congruence and information asymmetries exist between cloud provider and user *an analogy was drawn* between cloud service relationships and principal-agent problems and thus the principal-agent theory was used as a theoretical lens for developing the cloud service relationship theory. The cloud provider and the user have different interests and goals. While cloud users want a high-quality service, providers foremost want to make profits. Therefore, certain mechanisms need to exist that align the interests of provider and user in cloud service relationships. Moreover, for the cloud user it is impossible to fully verify the provider's true qualities and actions at any point in time and there can be a

Table 5.1 Research framework and cloud service relationship theory

Heuristic	Use of heuristic in developing cloud service relationship theory
"Making an assumption"	Uncertainty is important new aspect for explaining user behavior in cloud service relationships
"Making an analogy"	Cloud service relationships can be described as principal-agent problem
"Challenge the obvious"	Rational choice assumption does not hold. Rather, cloud users' behavior is bounded by the aspiration level they have on a satisfactory cloud service alternative. Moreover, beyond signals and incentives, social influence processes affect the evaluation of the cloud service
"Laundry-list"	NA
"Instantiation"	NA

significant time lag until users recognize reduction in promised service quality. In some case, the hidden actions of the provider may even never be detected.

In situations of goal congruence and information asymmetries, two agency problems exist. On the one hand, cloud users face a pool of focal and alternative cloud services and cannot differentiate between high quality and low quality cloud providers (Akerlof 1970). This situation is termed adverse selection problem. On the other hand, once the cloud user has transferred his or her data to the cloud provider, the cloud provider can potentially engage in hidden actions at the cloud user's expense (Jensen and Meckling 1976). This problem is termed moral hazard problem. Drawing on principal-agent theory, agency problems were assumed to represent distinct, persistent and concurrent problems in cloud service relationships. Further, positivist principal-agent theorists suggest that signals and incentives can be used to overcome these agency problems because they can align the interest of cloud user and provider as well as reduce information asymmetries between both parties (Eisenhardt 1989b). Therefore, these bilateral mechanisms were assumed to also mitigate uncertainties in cloud service relationships.

Third, *two assertions were challenged* of principal-agent theory in order to extend the theory to this new theoretical context. On the one hand, the assumption that all cloud users act rational and evaluate the full set of potential alternative cloud services. Rather, the theory assumes that cloud users are bounded rational in their decision-making given that cloud services are complex technologies and the potential value of using them is hard to predict. Drawing on bounded rationality theory (Simon 1955), it is assumed that cloud users differ in their aspiration level on a satisfactory cloud service alternative. The less knowledge about and interest in alternative cloud service users have, the less are uncertainties incorporated into their behavior. Therefore, it is assumed that cloud users' rationality is bounded by the aspiration level they have on a satisfactory cloud service alternative. On the other hand, it is assumed that the theory needs to integrate the social context of the users to fully understand users' evaluation of agency costs (Wiseman et al. 2012). Drawing on social influence theory (Kelman 1961), a social perspective was formally incorporated into the cloud service relationship theory. Via internalization, cloud users are influenced by the verbally expressed opinions of their social peers. Via identification, the behavior of referent others is incorporated into the evaluation of the cloud service (Wang et al. 2013). Hence, social influence mechanisms of internalization and identification mitigate agency problems in cloud service relationships.

Based on IS research and practitioner literature, operational manifestations of the theoretical constructs were subsequently developed in the form of observable variables. Three cloud-specific manifestations of agency problems in cloud service relationships were identified. On the one hand, privacy and security concerns arise because cloud users transfer sensitive data to the cloud provider and cannot evaluate whether the provider has the qualities to protect the data (security concerns) and whether the provider uses the data for secondary purposes or discloses the data to third parties without users' consent (privacy concerns). On the other hand, availability concerns arise from the commitment to and resulting dependence on the cloud provider's service. Due to information asymmetries, the cloud user can hardly evaluate whether the provider has sufficient resources and capacities to guarantee a high level of service availability.

Building on experience from e-commerce research, three bilateral mechanisms were identified that mitigate agency cost in cloud service relationships. First, the theory assumes that users who are exposed to a clear and visible website that conveys relevant information needed for evaluating the service have lower agency costs (Pavlou et al. 2007). Therefore the concepts of product diagnosticity and website informativeness were extended to the new theoretical context. Second, third-party assurances were proposed to represent differently costly and credible quality signalling mechanisms (Dimoka et al. 2012). Therefore, they were expected to be effective in mitigating cloud users' uncertainties. Third, the theory proposes that the anticipated legal sanctions can align the interest of cloud providers and users (Peace et al. 2003). While cloud-SLAs rarely entail any financial rewards, anticipated sanctions of violating SLAs were expected to reduce agency costs.

In order to characterize cloud users with low and high aspiration level, the theory assumes that knowledge about and interest in alternative cloud services can approximate groups with different aspiration levels on a satisfactory cloud service alternative. Thereby high knowledge about and high interest in alternative cloud service are both associated with high aspiration levels on a satisfactory alternative and vice versa. Further, WOM—a popular marketing concept—was used to operationalize internalization processes (Hennig-Thurau et al. 2002). Thereby, positive and negative word-of-mouth influences uncertainty evaluations of cloud users. In turn, peer adoption was used as a variable for operationalizing social influence processes of identification (Wang et al. 2013). The more friends and colleagues use cloud services, the lower cloud users' uncertainty evaluation.

Overall, the cloud service relationship theory meets all quality criteria for a theoretical contribution. The cloud service relationship theory represents a theoretical system of constructs and variables in which constructs are related to each other by propositions and the variables are related to each other by hypotheses (Bacharach 1989). It provides predictions and has both testable propositions and causal explanations. Therefore, the cloud service relationship theory can be assessed as an IS theory for explaining and predicting and thus conforms to the structural nature of theories in IS (Gregor 2006). It also entails all four essential elements of a theory as suggested by positivist theory-development authorities (Whetten 1989). First, it provides a comprehensive, parsimonious and cloud-specific set of factors that explain how uncertainties arise in cloud service relationships and how they can be mitigated. Second, the theory states how the identified sets of factors are interrelated. Third, it offers a clear and thorough rationale for justifying the section of variables and relationships. Lastly, it clearly articulates the boundary assumptions of the theory. Beyond being a complete theory, the cloud service relationship theory extends the extant knowledge about IS by integrating uncertainty considerations of users into the nomological network of IT user behavior. The theory development processes highlights how three heuristics can be utilized to choose ("Making an

Assumption"), instantiate ("Making an Analogy") and extend ("Challenge the Obvious") a well-established theory to a new theoretical IT innovation context.

5.3 Evaluating a Cloud Service Relationship Theory

The first challenge for evaluating theories on emerging IT innovations is to find suitable application scenarios where the characteristics of cloud services (e.g., on demand self-service, no up-front commitment, Armbrust et al. 2010) actually apply. Since cloud storage services are widely adopted by internet users and embody the typical features of cloud services, the cloud service relationship theory was evaluated based on an online survey among German Dropbox users, the market-leading cloud storage service in Germany.

Whether high quality Dropbox user survey statistics was obtained from the survey can be assessed using the framework of Groves et al. (2009) (Fig. 5.1). The framework assumes that two separate inferential steps are necessary in surveys. On the one hand, surveys aim for inferring from a response of a single participant to the true value of an underlying construct (Groves and Lyberg 2010). Thereby, measurement errors and a lack of content validity can threaten valid inferences from the measurement to the construct. Both content validity and correct measurements were ensured through the comprehensive scale development study (MacKenzie et al. 2011). Besides prevention, internal consistency reliability, discriminant validity, and convergent validity as well as the likelihood that CMV biases the results was assessed through a comprehensive measurement model evaluation (Hair et al. 2014). Based on the results, it can be concluded that measurement errors did not bias the path estimates and significance levels.

Besides inferences from a response of a single participant to the true value of an underlying construct, surveys at the same time aim for inferring from a set of respondents to a target population through statistical generalization (Groves et al. 2009). Thereby, coverage, sampling, non-response and adjustment errors can threaten valid inferences from the set of respondents to the target population.

Since a representative set of internet users was surveyed, coverage error and sampling errors should not bias the results. A coverage error occurs if the target population does not coincide with the population actually sampled, whereas the sampling error occurs if sample estimates differ from the true values of the population (Groves and Lyberg 2010). The only problematic aspect of the sample is that respondents are all members of an online panel. Since prior research suggests e.g., that panel participants adopt technology earlier than other survey respondents (Duffy et al. 2005), the obtained statistics might deviate from parameters of the population.

Moreover, two recommended tests controlling for a non-response error were conducted. A non-response error biases results if respondents are systematically different from those who did not participate in the survey. As recommended by methodologists, it was assumed that late respondents are similar to non-respondents

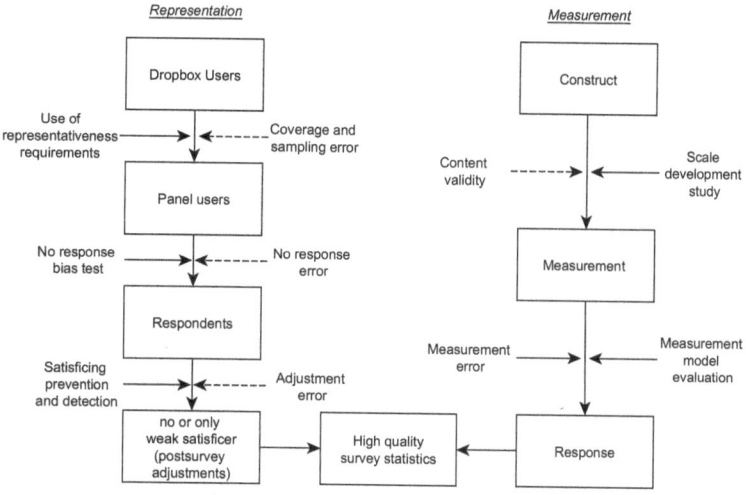

Fig. 5.1 Framework for quality survey statistics (cf. Groves et al. 2009)

and path estimates and significance levels were compared among both groups (Armstrong and Overton 1977). Since no significant differences were identified, it was concluded that a non-response bias did not bias the results.

Finally, online surveys are particularly vulnerable to satisficing behavior of respondents (Barge and Gehlbach 2012). Therefore, several measures were used to detect strong satisficers which were subsequently deleted from the final sample (adjustment error). Since no measure exists to evaluate whether satisficers are systematically different to non-satisficers, an estimate whether the path estimates are biased by the elimination of satisficers cannot be provided. However, anecdotal evidence that satisficers and non-satisficers are not systematically different is provided by Oppenheimer et al. (2009) who disciplined non-diligent respondents and did not find any systematic differences to non-satisficers. Overall, the systematic framework that links the steps of survey design, collection and estimation into error sources shows that the study controls for all important error sources (Groves and Lyberg 2010). Therefore, path estimates and significance level should be generalizable to the entire population of cloud storage service (especially Dropbox) users.

Given that reliable and valid measurement instruments were used, the key findings of the structural model evaluation can be summarized as follows: First, data-related concerns such as privacy and security concerns are the major sources of uncertainty in the context of cloud storage services, while dependency-related concerns (availability concerns) only play a marginal role. Second, cloud users with low knowledge about and interest in alternative cloud service may have privacy concerns, but do not fully incorporate privacy concerns into their evaluation of the service. In contrast, quality concerns (security and availability concerns) are equally incorporated among cloud users with a low and high aspiration level on a satisfactory cloud service alternative. Third, service diagnosticity and third-party assurances are the most effective measures to mitigate agency costs, whereas incentives hardly influence uncertainty evaluations of cloud users. Fourth, apart from bilateral mechanisms, users' evaluation is shaped in important ways by the opinions of their social peers. WOM of either valence influences the evaluation of cloud services. Thereby, cloud users place different weights on positive and negative opinions in making evaluations. Negative opinions have stronger influence than positive opinions. With the accumulation of service experience cloud users more strongly focus on their own judgment or concrete reference opinions about the qualities and actions of the cloud provider (Venkatesh and Morris 2000), rather than the behavior of relevant peers. The study shows that peer adoption does not influence cloud users' evaluation of the service.

Overall, the theory development and testing study contributes to IS in several ways. Extending principal-agent theory using multiple theories (Eisenhardt 1989a), the study contributes by developing and empirically validating a theory that explains how uncertainties arise and how they can be mitigated in ongoing cloud service relationships. Thereby different sources of uncertainty are disentangled and linked into the nomological network of IT user behavior.

Beyond, the study refines the understanding of the role of bounded rationality in cloud service relationships. Thereby, first empirical evidence and an explanation for the 'privacy paradox' are provided which has yet not been linked to IT service user behavior (Acquisti 2004). Moreover, the study sheds light on the role of different safeguarding mechanisms in cloud service relationships. On the one hand, the study confirms the important role of signals for reducing information asymmetries in online exchange environments. While quality signaling mechanisms are very important (Dimoka et al. 2012; Özpolat et al. 2013), incentives only play a marginal role. On the other hand, the study reveals that while internalization-based social influence processes have a persistent role for cloud users' evaluation of the service, the role of identification-based social influence processes seems to diminish with the accumulation of service experience.

5.4 Future Research

Cloud service relationships may well be an "extremely large, undiscovered, arena for future IS research" (Baskerville 2011, p. 253). This dissertation lays a solid foundation for future research on sociotechnical phenomena surrounding this field. Overall, I see two major pillars for future research on cloud services (Table 5.2).

On the one hand, I suggest elaborating on the methods ("how") for developing and empirically evaluating cloud theories. The research framework for theorizing entails a parsimonious but yet not necessarily comprehensive set of heuristics used for theorizing about cloud services. I believe that future research should also explore and compare heuristics previously used for theorizing about other IS fashion waves such as application service provisioning or outsourcing in order to find additional heuristics that can be used for theorizing about cloud services. Based

Table 5.2 Cloud research agenda

How	*Theory development (generalize research framework)*		
	Explore and compare heuristics used for theorizing about other IS fashion waves		
	Benchmark which heuristics are more "successful"		
	Explore sequences of heuristics used for theorizing about IS fashion waves		
	Theory evaluation (address online respondents' satisficing behavior)		
	Develop additional satisficing prevention techniques		
	Examine the extent to which satisficing behavior biases empirical results		
Where	*Cloud service relationships (user-side)*	*Cloud service relationships (enterprise-side)*	*Cloud service relationships (provider-side)*
	Retest theory for other cloud services	Examine how individual differences with respect to cloud service outcome can be overcome	Examine how cloud service relationships can become viable (w.r.t. user base and revenue streams)
	Examine explanatory power of theory over time (e.g., non-user/user)		

on this extended examination, cloud research could benefit from heuristics successfully applied in other research streams. Moreover, taking a more comprehensive set of articles, future research should also try to benchmark heuristics to examine which of them are more successful (e.g., in terms of publication outlet or long-term impact) (Colquitt and Zapata-Phelan 2007). As I have learned from the theory development process, heuristics are often used in a sequence. Therefore, future research should also explore and evaluate common sequences of heuristics to guide and improve future cloud theory development processes.

Apart from theory development, the way cloud theories are empirically evaluated should be improved. One of the major challenges of evaluating the cloud service relationship theory was satisficing behavior of respondents. IS research only provides limited standards for both preventing and detecting respondents' satisficing behavior. Given that cloud studies are predestinated to use online surveys and that IS researchers are especially knowledgeable about the particularities of the digital channel, I encourage future cloud research to develop techniques for preventing satisficing behavior which go beyond the comprehensive measures employed in the empirical study. Since many IS and cloud studies rely on online surveys, IS research should also examine—e.g., based on experiments or meta-analyses—the extent to which respondents' satisficing behavior biases empirical evaluations and how the elimination of strong satisficers from the final survey statistic biases results.

Building on these improved methods for theorizing and evaluation, I suggest advancing the knowledge about cloud service relationships in three major areas ("where"). First, researchers should re-test the cloud service relationship theory under different spatial and temporal conditions. Apart from cloud storage services, cloud service relationship should also be studied in the context of other common cloud services such as customer relationship management or enterprise resource planning services (spatial). Based on these empirical evaluations, researchers will be able to better describe the boundary conditions of the cloud service relationship theory. Moreover, the role of bilateral and social safeguarding mechanisms should be evaluated over the whole life-cycle of the cloud service relationship (temporal). As a first step, the explanatory power of the cloud service relationship theory for users and non-users of cloud services should be compared. Longitudinal studies could allow for better understanding post-adoption evaluations and behavior of cloud users over time.

Second, because previous cloud research places particular emphasis on the risks enterprises face when cloud services enter organizational boundaries, future research should also look at the positive individual and organizational effects of cloud services. More precisely, future research should examine whether inequalities with respect to individually adopted cloud service outcomes occur and how these differences can be best overcome by enterprises. For theorizing about the cloud divide, I suggest that this potential research stream should borrow knowledge from previous research on inequalities in the digital age.

Third, future research should also guide practice by explaining how cloud services can become self-sustainable with respect to the user base and revenues it generates. Because cloud services are an important growth market, cloud providers often focus on establishing a large customer base in the first place. In the long run however, they often lack a strategy to generate sufficient revenue streams. Therefore, future research should examine why some users stay, why some users leave, why some users spread the word about the service, why some users turn into profitable users while others do not.

Overall, I agree with Richard Baskerville who sees high potential for cloud research to extend the current knowledge about IS both methodologically and theoretically. Given that cloud services are fundamentally changing IT practice, I believe that cloud research is just at the beginning of understanding the changes induced by cloud services for the management of IS within and beyond enterprise boundaries.

Appendix A
Literature Analysis

The top journals of the discipline (*European Journal of Information Systems (EJIS)*, *Information Systems Journal (ISJ)*, *Information Systems Research (ISR)*, *Journal of AIS (JAIS)*, *Journal of Information Technology (JIT)*, *Journal of MIS (JMIS)*, *Journal of Strategic Information Systems (JSIS)*, *MIS Quarterly (MISQ)*), as well as the proceedings of the six leading IS conferences (*International Conference of Information Systems (ICIS)*, *European Conference of Information Systems (ECIS)*, *Hawaii International Conference on Systems Sciences (HICSS)*, *Americas' Conference on Information Systems (AMCIS)*, *Internationale Tagung Wirtschaftsinformatik (WI)*, *Multi-Konferenz Wirtschaftsinformatik (MKWI)*) have been evaluated with respect to mentioning the terms "Cloud", "SaaS", or "Software-as-a-Service" in abstract or title in the period 2007 till 2013. In total, 206 articles were identified. In the second step, only articles that can be counted to the positivist research paradigm were selected, i.e., only those articles that exhibit a behavioral science approach, apply the hypothetical-deductive logic, and validate the hypotheses empirically. By the end, the following 36 articles were deemed relevant for the subsequent in-depth analysis (Table A.1).

© Springer International Publishing Switzerland 2015
J. Huntgeburth, *Developing and Evaluating a Cloud Service Relationship Theory*,
Progress in IS, DOI 10.1007/978-3-319-10280-1

Table A.1 Literature analysis

#	Author	Year	Outlet	Title	Short Description
1	Huang, Ke-Wie; Wang, Mengdi	2009	ICIS	Firm-level productivity analysis for software as a service companies	Compare product functions of pure, mixed and non-SaaS providers
2	Benlian, Alexander	2009	ECIS	A transaction cost theoretical analysis of software-as-a-service (SAAS)-based sourcing in SMBs and enterprises	Examine the influence of transaction costs on the degree of SaaS outsourcing
3	Susarla, Anjana; Barua, Anitesh; and Whinston, Andrew B.	2009	JMIS	A transaction cost perspective of the "Software as a Service" business model	Examine how the contract design influences the SaaS partnership
4	Benlian, Alexander; Hess, Thomas	2009	WI	Welche Treiber lassen SaaS auch in Großunternehmen zum Erfolg werden?	Examine the influence of transaction costs on the degree of SaaS outsourcing
5	Benlian, Alexander; Hess, Thomas	2010	ECIS	The risks of sourcing software as a service —an empirical analysis of adopters and non-adopters	Examine the influence of different risk types on the degree of SaaS outsourcing
6	Koehler, Philip; Anandasivam, Arun; Dan, MA	2010	AMCIS	Cloud services from a consumer perspective	Examine customer preferences with respect to different characteristics of cloud services
7	Ramireddy, Srilakshmi; Chakraborthy, Rajarshi; Raghu, T.S.; Rao, H. Raghav	2010	AMCIS	Privacy and security practices in the Arena of cloud computing—a research in progress	Compare assurances of cloud provider among different types of cloud services
8	Koehler, Philip; Anandasivam, Arun, Dan, M. A.; Weinhardt, Christof	2010	ICIS	Customer heterogeneity and tariff biases in cloud computing	Examine customer preferences with respect to different characteristics of cloud services
9	Saya, S.; Pee, L. G.; Kankanhalli., A.	2010	ICIS	The impact of institutional influences on perceived technological characteristics and real options in cloud computing adoption	Examine the effect of different institutional pressures on the perceptions and intention to adopt cloud computing
10	Benlian, Alexander; Koufaris, Marios; und Hess, Thomas	2010	ICIS	The role of saas service quality for continued saas use: empirical insights from saas using firms	Examine different dimensions of SaaS service quality and ist influence of continuance

(continued)

Table A.1 (continued)

#	Author	Year	Outlet	Title	Short Description
11	Susarla, Anjana; Barua, Anitesh and Whinston, Andrew B.	2010	JMIS	Multitask agency, modular architecture, and task disaggregation in SaaS	Examine how cloud provider design contracts with customers
12	Lehmann, Sonja; Draisbach, Tobias; Koll, Corina; Buxmann, Peter; and Diefenbach, Heiner	2010	MKWI	Preisgestaltung für software-as-a-service	Examine customer preferences with respect to payment model
13	Winkler, Till; Goebel, Christoph; Benlian, Alexander; Bidault, Francis; Günther, Oliver	2011	ICIS	The impact of software as a service on IS authority—a contingency perspective	Examine how the allocation of decision-making responsibilities is dependent on the characteristics of SaaS services
14	Parameswaran, Srikanth; Venkatesan, Srikanth; Gupta, Manish; Sharman, Raj; and Rao, H. Raghav	2011	AMCIS	Impact of cloud computing announcements on firm valuation	Examine the effect of cloud adoption announcements on the stock market price of the focal firm and its competitors
15	Sun, Jia; und Wang, Ping	2012	ICIS	Community ecology for innovation concept: the case of cloud computing	In the context of cloud computing, they examine why concepts become popular and how they influence the deployment of IT in organizations
16	Winkler, Till J.; und Benlian, Alexander	2012	ICIS	The dual role of IS specificity in governing software as a service	Examine the effect of different dimensions of specificity on the governance of SaaS
17	Li, Yuan; und Chang, Kuo-chung	2012	AMCIS	A study on user acceptance of cloud computing: a multi-theoretical perspective	Examine the effect of different cloud success factors on the intention to adopt cloud computing
18	Malladi, Suresh; und Krishnan, Mayuram	2012	AMCIS	Does Software-as-a-Service (SaaS) has a role in IT-enabled innovation?—an empirical analysis	Examine the effect of SaaS usage on the innovativeness of a company
19	Bernius, Steffen; und Krönung, Julia	2012	ECIS	Fostering academic research by cloud computing—the users' perspective	Apply TAM to the cloud context

(continued)

Table A.1 (continued)

#	Author	Year	Outlet	Title	Short Description
20	Opitz, N.; Langkau, T.F.; Schmidt, N.H.; und Kolbe, L.M.	2012	HICSS	Technology acceptance of cloud computing: empirical evidence from german IT departments	Apply TAM 2 to understand cloud use
21	Retana, German F.; Forman, Chris; Narasimhan, Sridhar; Florin, Marius; und Niculescu, D. J. Wu	2012	ICIS	Technical support and IT capacity demand: evidence from the cloud	Examine the effect of technical support on the resource requirements of cloud customers
22	Malladi, Suresh; und Krishnan, Mayuram S.	2012	ICIS	Cloud computing adoption and its implications for CIO strategic focus—an empirical analysis	Examine how cloud adoption helps CIOs to focus more on strategic question
23	Ackermann, Tobias; Widjaja, Thomas; Benlian, Alexander; und Buxmann, Peter	2012	ICIS	Perceived IT security risks of cloud computing: conceptualization and scale development	Examine different dimensions of cloud security risks
24	Benlian, Alexander, Koufaris, Marios and Hess, Thomas	2012	JMIS	Service quality in software-as-a-service: developing the saas-qual measure and examining its role in usage continuance	Examine different dimension of SaaS service quality and its influence on the continued use of SaaS services
25	Kim, Kibae; Altmann, Jörn; und Lee, Wool-Rim	2013	ECIS	Patterns of innovation in saas networks: trend analysis of node centralities	Examine the development of innovation networks in the context of cloud computing
26	Walther, Sebastian; Sarker, Saonee; Sedera, Darshana; Otto, Boris; und Wunderlich, Philipp	2013	AMCIS	Exploring subscription renewal intention of operational cloud enterprise systems—a stakeholder perspective	Examine the effect of IS success on cloud continuance
27	Kung, LeeAnn, Cegielski, Casey; und Kung, Hsiang-Jui	2013	AMCIS	Environmental pressure on software as a service adoption: an integrated perspective	Examine the influence of institutional isomorphism on the adoption of cloud computing
28	Lansing, Jens; Schneider, Stephan; und Sunyaev, Ali	2013	ECIS	Cloud service certifications: measuring consumers' preferences for assurances	Examine different security mechanisms in the context of cloud computing

(continued)

Table A.1 (continued)

#	Author	Year	Outlet	Title	Short Description
29	Walterbusch, Marc; Martens, Benedikt; und Teuteberg, Frank	2013	ECIS	Exploring trust in cloud computing: a multi-method approach	Examine various trust-building mechanisms in the cloud context
30	Walther, Sebastian; Sarker, Saonee; Sedera, Darshana; und Eymann, Torsten	2013	ECIS	Exploring subscription renewal intention of operational cloud enterprise systems—a socio-technical approach	Examine the impact of cloud service success on cloud service continuance
31	Walther, Sebastian; Sedera, Darshana; Sarker, Saonee; und Eymann, Torsten	2013	ECIS	Evaluating operational cloud enterprise system success: an organizational perspective	Examine Cloud Service success
32	Trenz, Manuel, Huntgeburth, Jan C., Veit, Daniel J.	2013	ECIS	The role of uncertainty in cloud computing continuance: antecedents, mitigators, and consequences	Examine the role of uncertainty on satisfaction and continuance
33	Bhattacherjee, Anol; und Park, Sang Cheol	2013	EJIS	Why end-users move to the cloud: a migration-theoretic analysis	Examine the migration of service in the cloud
34	Coursaris, Constantinos K.; van Osch, Wietske; Sung, Jieun	2013	HICSS	A "Cloud Lifestyle": the diffusion of cloud computing applications and the effect of demographic and lifestyle clusters	Examine the effects of perceived innovation properties on the adoption intention in the context of cloud services
35	Borgman, Hans P.; Bahli, Bouchaib; Heier, Hauke; Schewski, Fiona	2013	HICSS	Cloudrise: exploring cloud computing adoption and governance with the TOE framework	Examining influencing factors of cloud adoption based on the TOE framework
36	Huntgeburth, Jan; Förderer, Jens; Ebertin, Cornelia, und Veit, Daniel	2013	WI	How cloud computing impacts stock market prices	Examine the effect of cloud announcements on the stock market price of the focal firm

Appendix B
Empirical Analysis

Measurement Instrument

Table B.1

© Springer International Publishing Switzerland 2015
J. Huntgeburth, *Developing and Evaluating a Cloud Service Relationship Theory*,
Progress in IS, DOI 10.1007/978-3-319-10280-1

Table B.1 Measurement models used in study (German version)

CONT1: Ich beabsichtige Dropbox eher weiter zu nutzen anstatt damit aufzuhören
CONT2: Mein Plan ist Dropbox weiter zu benutzen anstatt damit aufzuhören
CONT3: Wenn ich könnte, würde ich Dropbox weiter nutzen
CONT4: Ich beabsichtige Dropbox in Zukunft nicht mehr zu benutzen. [reverse]
SEC1: Dropbox trifft die nötigen Sicherheitsvorkehrungen, um meine Daten vor Angriffen von außerhalb zu schützen. [r]
SEC2: Dropbox stellt generell sicher, dass meine Informationen vor Hacker-Angriffen geschützt sind. [reverse]
SEC3: Ich fühle mich sicher, wenn ich Transaktionen mit Dropbox tätige.[reverse]
SEC4: Ich fühle mich sicher, wenn ich Informationen zu Dropbox transferiere.[reverse]
PRIV1: Ich befürchte, dass Dropbox meine persönlichen Daten ohne meine Erlaubnis für andere Zwecke verwendet
PRIV2: Ich befürchte, dass Dropbox meine persönlichen Daten ohne meine Erlaubnis für andere Zwecke weitergibt
PRIV3: Ich befürchte, dass Dropbox zu viele Daten über mich sammelt
PRIV4: Ich habe Bedenken bzgl. meiner Privatsphäre, wenn ich Dropbox nutze
AVA1: Ich habe Bedenken hinsichtlich der Verfügbarkeit von Dropbox
AVA2: Ich habe Bedenken, dass Dropbox vorübergehend nicht verfügbar sein könnte
AVA3: Ich bin beunruhigt, dass Dropbox kurzfristig unerreichbar ist
AVA4: Ich habe Zweifel daran, ob Dropbox jederzeit zuverlässig die Abrufbarkeit meiner Daten sicherstellen kann
AVA5: Meine Daten könnten vorübergehend nicht verfügbar sein, wenn sie bei Dropbox gespeichert werden
DIA1: Ich denke, dass ein Besuch der Webseite von Dropbox mir hilft, die Qualitäten des Dienstes zu beurteilen
DIA2: Ich denke, dass ein Besuch der Webseite von Dropbox mir hilft, mich mit den Qualitäten des Dienstes vertraut zu machen
DIA3: Ich denke, dass ein Besuch der Webseite von Dropbox mir hilft, die Qualitäten des Dienstes zu verstehen
DIA4: Ich denke, dass ein Besuch der Webseite von Dropbox mir ein gutes Gefühl dafür gibt, was der Dienst leistet
TPA1: Dropbox verfügt über qualitativ hochwertige Zertifikate von glaubwürdigen Akkreditierungsinstitutionen
TPA2: Dropbox kann beeindruckende Referenzen Dritter vorweisen
TPA3: Es gibt viele achtbare Zertifizierungen durch Dritte, die die Vertrauenswürdigkeit von Dropbox bestätigen
TPA4: Die Referenzen von Dropbox sind beeindruckend
Würde Dropbox dabei erwischt, gegen die Service-Level-Vereinbarungen (*) zu verstoßen, ...
LS1: ... wären die rechtlichen Konsequenzen sehr hoch
LS2: ... würden sie stark bestraft werden
LS3: ... wäre die Bestrafung schwerwiegend
LS4: ... würde Dropbox abgestraft werden
PWOM1: Andere haben sich mir gegenüber positiv über Dropbox geäußert

(continued)

| PWOM2: Leute, deren Rat ich gesucht habe, haben mir Dropbox empfohlen |
| PWOM3: Meine Freunde haben mich zu Dropbox eingeladen |
| PWOM4: Meine Freunde und Kollegen haben mir Dropbox empfohlen |
| NWOM1: Meine Freunde und Verwandte haben mich vor Dropbox gewarnt |
| NWOM2: Meine Freunde und Verwandte haben sich bei mir über Dropbox beklagt |
| NWOM3: Meine Freunde und Verwandte haben gesagt, dass ich Dropbox nicht nutzen soll |
| NWOM4: Andere haben sich mir gegenüber negativ über Dropbox geäußert |
| PAD1: Viele meiner Freunde und Kollegen nutzen Dropbox |
| PAD2: Dropbox ist unter meinen Freunden und Kollegen weit verbreitet |
| PAD3: Wenn Freunde und Kollegen einen Cloud-Speicher-Dienst nutzen, dann ist es meistens Dropbox |
| PAD4: Dropbox wird von meinen Freunden und Kollegen häufig zur Datensicherung und zum Datenaustausch genutzt |
| KNOW1: Ich verstehe, wie Cloud-Technologie funktioniert |
| KNOW2: Ich habe ein gutes Verständnis dafür, wie Cloud Technologie arbeitet |
| KNOW3: Ich kann die technischen Hintergründe von Cloud-Diensten leicht beschreiben |
| KNOW4: Es fällt mir leicht wiederzugeben, wie Cloud Technologie funktioniert |
| ATT1: Ich werde mich über Alternativen zu Dropbox informieren |
| ATT2: Neben Dropbox, werde ich hin und wieder andere Cloud-Speicher-Dienste ausprobieren |
| ATT3: Ich interessiere mich für Alternativen zu Dropbox |
| ATT4: Ich habe kein Interesse an anderen Cloud-Speicher-Diensten außer Dropbox. [reverse] |

Descriptives and Item-To-Construct Loadings

Table B.2

Multigroup Analyses

Tables B.3, B.4, B.5, B.6 and B.7.

Table B.2 Descriptives and loadings (item-to-construct-level)

Item	Descriptives		Outer and cross loadings									
	Mean	Std.	AVA	CONT	DIA	LS	PAD	PRIV	SEC	TPA	NWOM	PWOM
CONT1	5.82	1.315	-0.154	**0.944**	0.280	0.159	0.315	-0.260	-0.357	0.257	-0.236	0.299
CONT2	5.78	1.368	-0.156	**0.948**	0.280	0.154	0.283	-0.267	-0.355	0.257	-0.272	0.280
CONT3	5.74	1.421	-0.168	**0.886**	0.244	0.139	0.232	-0.212	-0.343	0.219	-0.279	0.233
CONT4	6.24	1.295	-0.187	**0.774**	0.188	0.113	0.167	-0.257	-0.264	0.195	-0.315	0.180
PWOM1	4.66	1.830	-0.140	0.29	0.243	0.121	0.415	-0.206	-0.275	0.316	-0.066	**0.883**
PWOM2	3.63	2.011	-0.054	0.237	0.146	0.161	0.362	-0.107	-0.227	0.294	0.086	**0.791**
PWOM4	4.33	2.109	-0.108	0.161	0.126	0.097	0.377	-0.167	-0.158	0.220	-0.017	**0.838**
NWOM1	1.59	1.133	0.255	-0.286	-0.166	-0.056	-0.032	0.275	0.158	-0.081	**0.895**	-0.018
NWOM2	1.65	1.182	0.25	-0.260	-0.118	-0.013	0.005	0.240	0.118	-0.067	**0.875**	0.003
NWOM3	1.73	1.308	0.243	-0.219	-0.092	-0.016	-0.010	0.242	0.128	-0.049	**0.825**	0.034
NWOM4	1.85	1.356	0.217	-0.284	-0.165	-0.082	-0.051	0.287	0.236	-0.099	**0.857**	-0.046
LS1	4.45	1.759	-0.058	0.137	0.334	**0.928**	0.099	-0.176	-0.297	0.336	-0.068	0.143
LS2	4.13	1.752	-0.042	0.142	0.327	**0.934**	0.090	-0.175	-0.328	0.354	-0.011	0.155
LS3	4.21	1.734	-0.046	0.148	0.354	**0.932**	0.103	-0.193	-0.318	0.360	-0.049	0.144
LS4	4.55	1.660	-0.067	0.158	0.369	**0.872**	0.068	-0.191	-0.329	0.332	-0.058	0.104
DIA1	4.59	1.457	-0.104	0.243	**0.892**	0.357	0.216	-0.265	-0.481	0.428	-0.107	0.203
DIA2	4.83	1.343	-0.118	0.233	**0.931**	0.367	0.196	-0.203	-0.440	0.393	-0.134	0.181
DIA3	4.77	1.347	-0.112	0.237	**0.926**	0.336	0.200	-0.216	-0.458	0.386	-0.123	0.174
DIA4	4.75	1.405	-0.119	0.309	**0.906**	0.323	0.233	-0.304	-0.478	0.387	-0.209	0.223
TPA1	4.24	1.258	-0.15	0.258	0.419	0.352	0.288	-0.297	-0.481	**0.957**	-0.087	0.310

(continued)

Table B.2 (continued)

Item	Descriptives		Outer and cross loadings									
	Mean	Std.	AVA	CONT	DIA	LS	PAD	PRIV	SEC	TPA	NWOM	PWOM
TPA2	4.16	1.289	-0.119	0.244	0.415	0.369	0.308	-0.268	-0.484	**0.956**	-0.066	0.321
TPA3	4.18	1.233	-0.140	0.235	0.414	0.361	0.278	-0.277	-0.501	**0.952**	-0.066	0.313
TPA4	4.24	1.295	-0.142	0.260	0.417	0.355	0.313	-0.295	-0.487	**0.946**	-0.111	0.331
PAD1	4.81	1.701	-0.074	0.253	0.214	0.121	**0.916**	-0.101	-0.162	0.276	0.003	0.428
PAD2	4.66	1.761	-0.095	0.262	0.185	0.078	**0.932**	-0.116	-0.176	0.301	0.002	0.43
PAD3	4.86	1.641	-0.108	0.266	0.195	0.064	**0.897**	-0.112	-0.166	0.264	-0.044	0.426
PAD4	4.60	1.691	-0.110	0.258	0.251	0.098	**0.913**	-0.119	-0.194	0.296	-0.055	0.406
PRIV1	3.47	1.766	0.503	-0.257	-0.252	-0.213	-0.113	**0.950**	0.491	-0.292	0.295	-0.182
PRIV2	3.45	1.786	0.505	-0.264	-0.283	-0.221	-0.104	**0.943**	0.512	-0.279	0.287	-0.179
PRIV3	3.65	1.819	0.514	-0.232	-0.215	-0.118	-0.128	**0.920**	0.477	-0.251	0.261	-0.191
PRIV4	3.57	1.771	0.514	-0.282	-0.263	-0.188	-0.115	**0.917**	0.531	-0.289	0.287	-0.184
SEC1	3.58	1.433	0.306	-0.331	-0.454	-0.321	-0.188	0.440	**0.912**	-0.496	0.150	-0.254
SEC2	3.88	1.544	0.317	-0.299	-0.453	-0.324	-0.130	0.450	**0.891**	-0.468	0.159	-0.172
SEC3	3.68	1.548	0.306	-0.344	-0.480	-0.296	-0.194	0.502	**0.904**	-0.459	0.165	-0.287
SEC4	3.55	1.486	0.371	-0.373	-0.458	-0.318	-0.179	0.560	**0.914**	-0.434	0.207	-0.259
AVA1	3.01	1.581	**0.917**	-0.183	-0.143	-0.070	-0.095	0.507	0.358	-0.138	0.276	-0.129
AVA2	3.18	1.695	**0.89**	-0.135	-0.108	-0.012	-0.074	0.465	0.294	-0.114	0.246	-0.096
AVA3	3.08	1.712	**0.860**	-0.13	-0.072	-0.014	-0.105	0.424	0.238	-0.095	0.218	-0.078
AVA4	3.24	1.670	**0.872**	-0.18	-0.147	-0.091	-0.117	0.541	0.382	-0.150	0.251	-0.154
AVA5	3.34	1.661	**0.785**	-0.156	-0.046	-0.051	-0.068	0.402	0.254	-0.121	0.215	-0.071

Table B.3 PLS-MGA (critical data)

| Hypothesis | Group 1 (critical data) | | | Group 2 (non-critical data) | | | Difference | | | Type |
	p(1)	se(p(1))	t(1)	p(2)	se(p(2))	t(2)	|p(1)–p(2)|	p value	
H1a: SEC->CONT	−0.301	0.0505	5.9631	−0.325	0.0435	7.4772	0.024	0.72	
H1b: PRIV->CONT	−0.125	0.0508	2.4559	−0.077	0.0527	1.4685	0.048	0.51	
H1c: AVA->CONT	−0.018	0.0507	0.3613	−0.024	0.0432	0.5599	0.006	0.93	
H4a: DIA->SEC	−0.219	0.0401	5.4544	−0.406	0.0398	10.1828	0.187	0.00	M
H4b: DIA->PRIV	−0.061	0.0469	1.3025	−0.154	0.0491	3.1311	0.093	0.17	
H4c: DIA->AVA	0.031	0.0493	0.6261	−0.077	0.0499	1.542	0.108	0.12	
H5a: TPA->SEC	−0.312	0.0453	6.8959	−0.285	0.0423	6.7327	0.027	0.66	
H5b: TPA->PRIV	−0.142	0.0438	3.244	−0.181	0.0477	3.7832	0.039	0.55	
H5c: TPA->AVA	−0.051	0.046	1.1135	−0.089	0.052	1.7092	0.038	0.58	
H6a: LS->SEC	−0.101	0.0437	2.3068	−0.113	0.0358	3.1582	0.012	0.83	
H6b: LS->PRIV	−0.102	0.0443	2.3108	−0.08	0.0431	1.8614	0.022	0.72	
H6c: LS->AVA	−0.011	0.0464	0.23	−0.003	0.0457	0.0649	0.008	0.90	
H7a: PWOM->SEC	−0.113	0.0399	2.8343	−0.09	0.0349	2.5829	0.023	0.66	
H7b: PWOM->PRIV	−0.175	0.0401	4.3717	−0.046	0.0423	1.0871	0.129	0.03	S
H7c: PWOM->AVA	−0.161	0.0441	3.6459	0.018	0.0529	0.3352	0.179	0.01	S
H8a: NWOM->SEC	0.08	0.0365	2.1827	0.156	0.03	5.1874	0.076	0.11	
H8b: NWOM->PRIV	0.254	0.0341	7.4509	0.293	0.0357	8.2207	0.039	0.43	
H8c: NWOM->AVA	0.285	0.0374	7.6158	0.259	0.0357	7.2405	0.026	0.61	

(continued)

Table B.3 (continued)

| Hypothesis | Group 1 (critical data) | | | Group 2 (non-critical data) | | | Difference | | Type |
	p(1)	se(p(1))	t(1)	p(2)	se(p(2))	t(2)	|p(1)–p(2)|	p value	
H9a: PAD->SEC	0.03	0.039	0.7598	0.04	0.0355	1.1341	0.01	0.85	
H9b: PAD->PRIV	-0.025	0.0388	0.6376	0.054	0.0435	1.2525	0.079	0.18	
H9c: PAD->AVA	0.008	0.0431	0.1924	-0.099	0.0487	2.0354	0.107	0.10	

Note M magnitude differences, D sign direction differences, S significance level difference

Table B.4 PLS-MGA (business vs. private use)

Hypothesis	Group 3 (private only)			Group 4 (business and private)			Difference		
	p(3)	se(p(3))	t(3)	p(4)	se(p(4))	t(4)	|p(3)-p(4)|	p value	Type
H1a: SEC->CONT	-0.374	0.0424	8.8183	-0.258	0.0494	5.2192	0.116	0.07	
H1b: PRIV->CONT	-0.072	0.0517	1.3972	-0.119	0.0521	2.2754	0.047	0.52	
H1c: AVA->CONT	0.007	0.0452	0.1647	-0.046	0.0507	0.9145	0.053	0.43	
H4a: DIA->SEC	-0.401	0.0388	10.3331	-0.192	0.0412	4.6559	0.209	0.00	M
H4b: DIA->PRIV	-0.227	0.0449	5.0657	0.032	0.0467	0.6882	0.259	0.00	S
H4c: DIA->AVA	-0.036	0.0482	0.7442	-0.011	0.0474	0.2356	0.025	0.71	
H5a: TPA->SEC	-0.256	0.0458	5.5952	-0.371	0.0387	9.5721	0.115	0.06	
H5b: TPA->PRIV	-0.136	0.0459	2.9584	-0.214	0.0449	4.7625	0.078	0.22	
H5c: TPA->AVA	-0.035	0.0508	0.6862	-0.177	0.047	2.4843	0.142	0.04	S
H6a: LS->SEC	-0.09	0.0366	2.4671	-0.1	0.0417	2.3921	0.01	0.86	
H6b: LS->PRIV	-0.064	0.0405	1.5839	-0.055	0.0451	1.2172	0.009	0.88	
H6c: LS->AVA	0.025	0.0443	0.5687	-0.001	0.0465	0.0298	0.026	0.69	
H7a: PWOM->SEC	-0.055	0.0375	1.4682	-0.155	0.039	3.9807	0.1	0.06	
H7b: PWOM->PRIV	-0.088	0.0408	2.1623	-0.153	0.0416	3.6822	0.065	0.26	
H7c: PWOM->AVA	-0.035	0.0449	0.7876	-0.144	0.0504	2.8463	0.109	0.11	
H8a: NWOM->SEC	0.086	0.0312	2.7528	0.13	0.034	3.8107	0.044	0.34	
H8b: NWOM->PRIV	0.246	0.0319	7.6964	0.282	0.0356	7.9213	0.036	0.45	
H8c: NWOM->AVA	0.249	0.0349	7.1356	0.258	0.0365	7.0645	0.009	0.86	
H9a: PAD->SEC	-0.017	0.033	0.5067	0.097	0.0409	2.3704	0.114	0.03	S
H9b: PAD->PRIV	0.028	0.0403	0.6892	-0.006	0.0408	0.1577	0.034	0.55	
H9c: PAD->AVA	-0.088	0.0452	1.9527	-0.002	0.0407	0.0595	0.086	0.16	

Note M magnitude differences, *D* sign direction differences, *S* significance level difference

Table B.5 PLS-MGA (young vs. old)

Hypothesis	Group 5 (young)			Group 6 (old)			Difference		Type
	p(5)	se(p(5))	t(5)	p(6)	se(p(6))	t(6)	|p(5)-p(6)|	p value	
H1a: SEC->CONT	−0.295	0.037	7.9646	−0.34	0.0608	5.5906	0.045	0.53	
H1b: PRIV->CONT	−0.134	0.0457	2.9341	−0.051	0.0616	0.8308	0.083	0.28	
H1c: AVA->CONT	0.053	0.0471	1.1184	−0.097	0.0474	2.0488	0.15	0.02	S
H4a: DIA->SEC	−0.213	0.0433	4.9219	−0.385	0.0399	9.6538	0.172	0.00	M
H4b: DIA->PRIV	−0.044	0.0452	0.9661	−0.214	0.0463	4.6294	0.17	0.01	S
H4c: DIA->AVA	−0.023	0.0474	0.4911	−0.038	0.0504	0.7569	0.015	0.83	
H5a: TPA->SEC	−0.255	0.0451	5.6614	−0.308	0.0439	7.0193	0.053	0.40	
H5b: TPA->PRIV	−0.145	0.046	3.1511	−0.15	0.045	3.3281	0.005	0.94	
H5c: TPA->AVA	0.048	0.0477	0.9958	−0.177	0.0517	3.4323	0.225	0.00	S
H6a: LS->SEC	−0.161	0.0441	3.6435	−0.082	0.0348	2.3475	0.079	0.16	
H6b: LS->PRIV	0.047	0.0417	1.1255	−0.19	0.0436	4.3608	0.237	0.00	S
H6c: LS->AVA	0.016	0.0494	0.3182	0.002	0.0444	0.0374	0.014	0.83	
H7a: PWOM->SEC	−0.12	0.0458	2.614	−0.115	0.0329	3.495	0.005	0.93	
H7b: PWOM->PRIV	−0.094	0.0478	1.9573	−0.121	0.0365	3.3156	0.027	0.65	
H7c: PWOM->AVA	−0.04	0.052	0.7769	−0.107	0.0432	2.4696	0.067	0.32	
H8a: NWOM->SEC	0.067	0.0257	2.6205	0.143	0.0393	3.6428	0.076	0.11	
H8b: NWOM->PRIV	0.265	0.0339	7.8215	0.263	0.0384	6.8534	0.002	0.97	
H8c: NWOM->AVA	0.311	0.036	8.6402	0.227	0.0385	5.9028	0.084	0.11	

(continued)

Table B.5 (continued)

| Hypothesis | Group 5 (young) | | | Group 6 (old) | | | Difference | | |
	p(5)	se(p(5))	t(5)	p(6)	se(p(6))	t(6)	|p(5)-p(6)|	p value	Type
H9a: PAD->SEC	−0.011	0.041	0.2802	0.065	0.0359	1.811	0.076	0.16	
H9b: PAD->PRIV	−0.088	0.0462	1.9008	0.114	0.0397	2.8603	0.202	0.00	D
H9c: PAD->AVA	−0.048	0.0439	1.0886	−0.019	0.045	0.4204	0.029	0.64	

Note M magnitude differences, *D* sign direction differences, *S* significance level difference

Table B.6 PLS-MGA (female vs. male)

Hypothesis	Group 7 (female)			Group 8 (male)				Difference		Type
	p(7)	se(p(7))	t(7)	p(8)	se(p(8))	t(8)	|p(7)–p(8)|	p value		
H1a: SEC->CONT	−0.212	0.0496	2.2571	−0.442	0.0404	10.9476	0.23	0.00	M	
H1b: PRIV->CONT	−0.097	0.0467	6.5123	0.03	0.0498	0.6057	0.127	0.06		
H1c: AVA->CONT	−0.047	0.0509	0.9664	−0.05	0.0451	1.107	0.003	0.96		
H4a: DIA->SEC	−0.212	0.0413	5.1232	−0.361	0.0409	8.821	0.149	0.01	M	
H4b: DIA->PRIV	−0.097	0.0449	2.1642	−0.12	0.0491	2.4515	0.023	0.73		
H4c: DIA->AVA	−0.006	0.0449	0.1396	−0.042	0.0515	0.8196	0.036	0.60		
H5a: TPA->SEC	−0.345	0.0456	7.5743	−0.267	0.0447	5.9689	0.078	0.22		
H5b: TPA->PRIV	−0.172	0.0426	4.0424	−0.167	0.0506	3.2948	0.005	0.94		
H5c: TPA->AVA	−0.074	0.0432	1.7246	−0.066	0.0546	1.2013	0.008	0.91		
H6a: LS->SEC	−0.111	0.0428	2.6018	−0.093	0.0361	2.5649	0.018	0.75		
H6b: LS->PRIV	−0.012	0.0428	0.2859	−0.096	0.0442	2.1769	0.084	0.17		
H6c: LS->AVA	−0.02	0.0468	0.4294	0.028	0.0449	0.628	0.048	0.46		
H7a: PWOM->SEC	−0.047	0.0449	1.0465	−0.148	0.0356	4.1554	0.101	0.08		
H7b: PWOM->PRIV	−0.127	0.0439	2.8956	−0.102	0.042	2.4318	0.025	0.68		
H7c: PWOM->AVA	0.002	0.0476	0.0385	−0.136	0.0472	2.8695	0.138	0.04	S	
H8a: NWOM->SEC	0.08	0.0357	2.2367	0.13	0.0324	4.0234	0.05	0.30		
H8b: NWOM->PRIV	0.31	0.0338	9.1728	0.246	0.0356	6.9134	0.064	0.19		
H8c: NWOM->AVA	0.305	0.0325	9.3855	0.255	0.0382	6.6814	0.05	0.32		

(continued)

Table B.6 (continued)

Hypothesis	Group 7 (female)			Group 8 (male)			Difference		
	p(7)	se(p(7))	t(7)	p(8)	se(p(8))	t(8)	|p(7)–p(8)|	p value	Type
H9a: PAD->SEC	0.098	0.0404	2.4167	0.002	0.0358	0.0595	0.096	0.08	
H9b: PAD->PRIV	0.022	0.0396	0.5588	0.027	0.0442	0.6055	0.005	0.93	
H9c: PAD->AVA	−0.032	0.0468	0.6908	−0.035	0.0451	0.7855	0.003	0.96	

Note M magnitude differences, D sign direction differences, S significance level difference

Table B.7 PLS-MGA (early vs. late respondents)

Hypothesis	Group 9 (early: N = 351)			Group 10 (late: N = 287)				Difference			Type
	p(9)	se(p(9))	t(9)	p(10)	se(p(10))	t(10)		|p(9)–p(10)|	p value		
H1a: SEC->CONT	−0.309	0.048	6.451	−0.315	0.0434	7.2613		0.006	0.93		
H1b: PRIV->CONT	−0.099	0.0559	1.7713	−0.095	0.0499	1.9044		0.004	0.96		
H1c: AVA->CONT	−0.064	0.051	1.2632	0.035	0.0436	0.8057		0.099	0.14		
H4a: DIA->SEC	−0.33	0.0413	7.9921	−0.281	0.0394	7.1482		0.049	0.39		
H4b: DIA->PRIV	−0.124	0.0483	2.5613	−0.107	0.0476	2.2424		0.017	0.80		
H4c: DIA->AVA	−0.077	0.0488	1.5846	0.049	0.0499	0.9924		0.126	0.07		
H5a: TPA->SEC	−0.356	0.0453	7.8563	−0.241	0.0443	5.4532		0.115	0.07		
H5b: TPA->PRIV	−0.195	0.05	3.9035	−0.137	0.0446	3.0716		0.058	0.39		
H5c: TPA->AVA	−0.064	0.05	1.2722	−0.077	0.0492	1.562		0.013	0.85		
H6a: LS->SEC	−0.114	0.0385	2.9518	−0.068	0.0411	1.6544		0.046	0.41		
H6b: LS->PRIV	−0.086	0.0451	1.9128	−0.025	0.0427	0.5922		0.061	0.33		
H6c: LS->AVA	−0.026	0.0497	0.5197	0.032	0.0434	0.7306		0.058	0.38		
H7a: PWOM->SEC	−0.065	0.0392	1.6657	−0.144	0.0398	3.6325		0.079	0.16		
H7b: PWOM->PRIV	−0.088	0.0421	2.098	−0.149	0.0438	3.3965		0.061	0.31		
H7c: PWOM->AVA	−0.119	0.049	2.4328	−0.045	0.0449	1.0129		0.074	0.27		
H8a: NWOM->SEC	0.076	0.0358	2.1338	0.17	0.0265	6.4245		0.094	0.03	M	
H8b: NWOM->PRIV	0.263	0.0358	7.3285	0.287	0.0324	8.8678		0.024	0.62		
H8c: NWOM->AVA	0.308	0.0387	7.9723	0.218	0.0338	6.4547		0.09	0.08		

(continued)

Table B.7 (continued)

| Hypothesis | Group 9 (early: N = 351) | | | Group 10 (late: N = 287) | | | Difference | | |
	p(9)	se(p(9))	t(9)	p(10)	se(p(10))	t(10)	|p(9)–p(10)|	p value	Type
H9a: PAD->SEC	0.035	0.0384	0.9067	0.045	0.0369	1.2222	0.01	0.85	
H9b: PAD->PRIV	0.003	0.0432	0.0649	0.072	0.0398	1.8131	0.069	0.24	
H9c: PAD->AVA	0.006	0.0437	0.1261	–0.1	0.0457	2.1963	0.106	0.09	

Note M magnitude differences, D sign direction differences, S significance level difference

References

Abbot, A. (2004). *Methods of discovery: heuristics for the social sciences*. New York, USA: W. W. Norton & Company.

Accenture (2010). *Cloud computing versus security and privacy: dark clouds?* Retrieved 20. January, 2014, from http://www.accenture-blogpodium.nl/technology/cloud-computing-versus-security-and-privacy-dark-clouds/.

Accenture (2011). *Consumer IT: The global workplace revolution has begun*. Retrieved 28. July, 2013, from http://www.accenture.com/SiteCollectionDocuments/Accenture-Consumerization-IT-Infographic.pdf.

Ackermann, T., Widjaja, T., Benlian, A., & Buxmann, P. (2012). Perceived IT security risks of cloud computing: conceptualization and scale development. In *Proceedings of the 33rd international conference on information systems* (pp. 45–63). Orlando: USA.

Acquisti, A. 2004. Privacy in Electronic Commerce and the Economics of Immediate Gratification. In *ACM Electronic commerce conference 2004 proceedings*, New York: USA.

AGOF (2013). *Internet facts 2013-03*. Retrieved 2. March, 2014, from http://www.agof.de/studienarchiv-internet-2013/.

Akerlof, G. A. (1970). The market for 'Lemons': Quality uncertainty and the market mechanism. *The Quarterly Journal of Economics, 84*(3), 488–500.

Anderson, E. W. (1998). Customer satisfaction and word of mouth. *Journal of Service Research, 1*(1), 5–17.

Armbrust, M., Stoica, I., Zaharia, M., Fox, A., Griffith, R., Joseph, A. D., et al. (2010). A view of cloud computing. *Communications of the ACM, 53*(4), 50–58.

Armstrong, J. S., & Overton, T. S. (1977). Estimating nonresponse bias in mail surveys. *Journal of Marketing Research, 14*(3), 396–402.

Arrow, K. J. (1963). Uncertainty and the welfare economics of medical care. *The American Economic Review, 53*(5), 941–973.

Association for Information Systems (2011). *Senior Scholars' Basket of Journals*. Retrieved 19. January, 2014, from http://start.aisnet.org/?SeniorScholarBasket.

Bacharach, S. B. (1989). Organizational theories: Some criteria for evaluation. *The Academy of Management Review, 14*(4), 496–515.

Bain & Company (2012). *Selling the cloud*. Retrieved 16. March, 2014, from http://www.bain.com/Images/BAIN_BRIEF_Selling_the_cloud.pdf.

Barge, S., & Gehlbach, H. (2012). Using the theory of satisficing to evaluate the quality of survey data. *Research in Higher Education, 53*(2), 182–200.

Baskerville, R. (2011). Individual information systems as a research arena. *European Journal of Information Systems, 20*(3), 251–254.

Baskerville, R. L., & Myers, M. D. (2009). Fashion waves in information systems research and practice. *MIS Quarterly, 33*(4), 647–662.

Belanger, F., & Crossler, R. (2011). Privacy in the digital age: a review of information privacy research in information systems. *MIS Quarterly, 35*(4), 1017–1041.

© Springer International Publishing Switzerland 2015

J. Huntgeburth, *Developing and Evaluating a Cloud Service Relationship Theory*, Progress in IS, DOI 10.1007/978-3-319-10280-1

Belanger, F., Hiller, J., & Smith, W. J. (2002). Trustworthiness in electronic commerce: The role of privacy, security, and site attributes. *Journal of Strategic Information Systems, 11*(3/4), 245–270.

Benbasat, I., & Zmud, R. W. (2003). The identity crisis within the is discipline: Defining and communicating the discipline's core properties. *MIS Quarterly, 27*(2), 183–194.

Bendapudi, N., & Berry, L. L. (1997). Customers' motivations for maintaining relationships with service providers. *Journal of Retailing, 73*(1), 15–37.

Benlian, A. (2009). A transaction cost theoretical analysis of software-as-a-service (SaaS)-based sourcing in smbs and enterprises. *Proceedings of the European Conference on Information Systems, (ECIS)*. Verona, Italy.

Benlian, A. & Hess, T. (2009). Welche Treiber lassen SaaS auch in Großunternehmen zum Erfolg werden? Eine empirische Analyse der SaaS-Adoption auf Basis der Transaktionskostentheorie," in Wirtschaftsinformatik 2009 Proceedings, Wien, Österreich.

Benlian, A. & Hess, T. (2010). The risks of sourcing software as a service—an empirical analysis of adopters and non-adopters. Proceedings of the European Conference on Information Systems, (ECIS). Pretoria, South Africa.

Benlian, A., Hess, T., & Buxmann, P. (2009). Drivers of SaaS-Adoption—An empirical study of different application types. *Business and Information Systems Engineering, 1*(5), 357–369.

Benlian, A., Koufaris, M., & Hess, T. (2010). The role of saas service quality for continued saas use: Empirical insights from saas using firms. In *ICIS 2010 proceedings*, St. Louis: USA.

Benlian, A., Koufaris, M., & Hess, T. (2011). Service quality in software-as-a-service: Developing the SaaS-Qual measure and examining its role in usage continuance. *Journal of Management Information Systems, 28*(3), 85–126.

Bernius, S., & Krönung, J. (2012). Fostering academic research by cloud computing—The users' perspective. In *ECIS 2012 proceedings*. Barcelona: Spain.

Bhattacherjee, A. (2001). Understanding information systems continuance: An expectation-confirmation model. *MIS Quarterly, 25*(3), 351–370.

Bhattacherjee, A., & Park, S. C. (2013). Why end-users move to the cloud: a migration-theoretic analysis. *European Journal of Information Systems, 22*(1), 1–16.

Bitcurrent (2011). *Bitcurrent cloud computing survey 2011*. Retrieved 29. April, 2012, from http://www.bitcurrent.com/download/cloud-computing-survey-2011/.

Bitkom (2012). *Die hightech-trends des Jahres 2012*. Retrieved 15. March, 2014, from http://www.bitkom.org/de/themen/77194_70999.aspx.

Blodgett, J. G., Hill, D. J., & Tax, S. S. (1997). The effects of distributive, procedural, and interactional justice on post complaint behavior. *Journal of Retailing, 73*(2), 185–210.

Borgman, H., Bahli, B., Heier, H., & Schewski, F. (2013) Cloudrise: Exploring cloud computing adoption and governance with the TOE framework. *Proceedings of the HICSS*. Maui, Hawaii, USA.

Boston Consulting Group (2009). *Capturing the value of cloud computing: How enterprises can chart their course to the next level*. Retrieved 20. January, 2014, from http://www.bcg.com/documents/file34246.pdf.

Bostrom, R. P., Gupta, S., & Thomas, D. (2009). A meta-theory for understanding information systems within sociotechnical systems. *Journal of Management Information Systems, 26*(1), 17–47.

Burton Group (2009). *Cloud computing: Transforming IT*. Retrieved 20. January, 2014, from http://www.gartner.com/technology/research/burton-group.jsp?cid=1681.

Buyya, R., Yeo, C. S., and Venugopal, S. (2008). Market-oriented cloud computing: vision, hype, and reality for delivering IT services as computing utilities. In *IEEE international conference on high performance computing and communications 2008 proceedings*, Dalian: China.

Campbell, D. T., & Fiske, D. W. (1959). Convergent and discriminant validation by the multitrait-multimethods matrix. *Psychological Bulletin, 56*(2), 81–105.

Carr, N. G. (2003). IT doesn't matter. *Harvard Business Review, 81*(5), 1–32.

Chalmers, A. F. (1999). *What is this thing called science?* (3rd ed.). St. Lucia, Australia: Mcgraw-Hill Higher Education.

Chen, W., & Hirschheim, R. (2004). A paradigmatic and methodological examination of information systems research from 1991 to 2001. *Information Systems Journal, 14*(3), 197–235.

Chin, W. W. (1998). Commentary: Issues and opinion on structural equation modeling. *MIS Quarterly, (22:1)*, vii–xvi.

Churchill, G. A. (1979). A paradigm for developing better measures of marketing constructs. *Journal of Marketing Research, 16*(1), 64–73.

Clemons, E. K., & Chen, Y. (2011). Making the decision to contract for cloud services: Managing the risk of an extreme form of IT outsourcing. *Proceedings of the HICSS.* Kauai, Hawaii, USA

Cohen, J. (1988). *Statistical power analysis for the behavior sciences.* Hillsdale, NJ, USA: Lawrence Erlbaum.

Colquitt, J. A., & Zapata-Phelan, C. P. (2007). Trends in theory building and theory testing: A five-decade study on the academy of management journals. *Academy of Management Journal, 50*(6), 1281–1303.

Coursaris, C., van Osch, W., & Sung, J. (2013). A 'Cloud Lifestyle': The diffusion of cloud computing applications and the effect of demographic and lifestyle clusters. *Proceedings of the HICSS.* Maui, Hawaii, USA

Crawford, V. P., & Sobel, J. (1982). Strategic information transmission. *Econometrica, 50*(6), 1431–1451.

Cronbach, L. J. (1951). Coefficient alpha and the internal structure of tests. *Psychometrika, 16*(3), 297–334.

D'Arcy, J., Hovav, A., & Galetta, D. (2009). User awareness of security countermeasures and its impact on information systems misuse: A deterrence approach. *Information Systems Research, 20*(1), 79–98.

Davis, J. H., Schoorman, F. D., & Donalsdon, L. (1997). Toward a stewardship theory of management. *Academy of Management Review, 22*(1), 20–47.

De Matos, C. A., & Rossi, C. A. V. (2008). Word-of-mouth communications in marketing: a meta-analytic review of the antecedents and moderators. *Journal of the Academy of Marketing Science, 36*(4), 578–596.

Deloitte (2009). *Cloud computing: Forecasting change.* Retrieved 16. March, 2014, from https://www.deloitte.com/assets/Dcom-Netherlands/Local%20Assets/Documents/EN/Services/Consulting/nl_en_consulting_cloud_computing_security_privacy_and_trust.pdf.

Der Spiegel (2013). *Edward snowden interview: The NSA and its willing helpers.* Retrieved 20. January, 2014, from http://www.spiegel.de/international/world/interview-with-whistleblower-edward-snowden-on-global-spying-a-910006.html.

Deutsche Bank Research (2012). *Cloud computing: Clear skies ahead.* Retrieved 20. January, 2014, from http://www.dbresearch.com/PROD/DBR_INTERNET_EN-PROD/PROD00000000 00285827.pdf.

Dibbern, J., Goles, T., Hirschheim, R., & Jayatilaka, B. (2004). Information systems outsourcing: A survey and analysis of the literature. *ACM SIGMIS Database, 35*(4), 6–102.

Dibbern, J., Winkler, J., & Heinzl, A. (2008). Explaining variations in client extra costs between software projects offshored to india. *MIS Quarterly, 32*(2), 333–366.

Dimoka, A., Hong, Y., & Pavlou, P. A. (2012). On product uncertainty in online markets: Theory and evidence. *MIS Quarterly, 36*(2), 395–426.

Duffy, B., Smith, K., Terhanian, G., & Bremer, J. (2005). Comparing data from online and face-to-face surveys. *International Journal of Market Research, 47*(6), 615–639.

Eagly, A. H., & Wood, W. (1982). Inferred sex differences in status as a determinant of gender stereotypes about social influence. *Journal of Personality and Social Psychology, 43*(5), 915–928.

Eisenhardt, K. M. (1989). Agency theory: An assessment and review. *The Academy of Management Review, 14*(1), 57–74.

Eisenhardt, K. M. (1989). Building theories from case study research. *The Academy of Management Review, 14*(4), 532–550.

Ermakova, T., Huenges, J., Erek, K., & Zarnekow, R. (2013). Cloud computing in healthcare—a literature review on current state of research. In *AMCIS 2013 proceedings*. Chicago:USA.

Ernst & Young (2011). *Cloud computing issues and impacts.* Retrieved 16. March, 2014, from http://www.ey.com/Publication/vwLUAssets/Cloud-computing_issues_and_impacts/$FILE/Cloud_computing_issues_and_impacts.pdf.

Ernst, C.-P. H., & Rothlauf, F. (2012). *Potenzielle Erfolgsfaktoren von SaaS-Unternehmen, In MKWI 2012 proceedings*. Germany: Braunschweig.

Fichman, R. G. (2004). Going beyond the dominant paradigm for information technology innovation research: Emerging concepts and methods. *Journal of the Association for Information Systems, 5*(8), 314–355.

Fishbein, M., & Ajzen, I. (1975). *Belief, Attitude, Intention, and Behavior: An introduction to theory and research*. Reading, USA: Addison-Wesley.

Fornell, C., & Larcker, D. F. (1981). Evaluating structural equation models with unobservable variables and measurement error. *Journal of Marketing Research, 18*(1), 39–50.

Forrest, W. (2009). *Clearing the air on cloud computing.* Retrieved 11. July, 2013, from http://www.cloudmagazine.fr/dotclear/public/clearing_the_air_on_cloud_computing.pdf.

Gartner (2008). *Assessing the security risks of cloud computing.* Retrieved 16. March, 2014, from https://www.gartner.com/doc/685308.

Gefen, D. (2002). Customer loyalty in E-Commerce. *Journal of the Association for Information Systems, 3*(1), 27–51.

Gefen, D., Rigdon, E., & Straub, D. (2011). An update and extension to SEM guidelines for administrative and social science research. *MIS Quarterly, (35:2)*, iii–A7.

Gefen, D., Wyss, S., & Lichtenstein, Y. (2008). Business familiarity as risk mitigation in software development outsourcing contracts. *MIS Quarterly, 32*(3), 531–551.

Gellman, B. B. (2013). Edward Snowden, after months of NSA revelations, says his mission's accomplished. In *Washington Post* Retrieved 20. January, 2014, from http://www.washington post.com/world/national-security/edward-snowden-after-months-of-nsa-revelations-says-his-missions-accomplished/2013/12/23/49fc36de-6c1c-11e3-a523-fe73f0ff6b8d_story.html.

Goo, J., Kishore, R., Rao, H. R., & Nam, K. (2009). The role of service level agreements in relational management of information technology outsourcing: An empirical study. *MIS Quarterly, 33*(1), 119–145.

Goodhue, D. L., Lewis, W., & Thompson, R. (2006). PLS, small sample size, and statistical power in mis research. *Proceedings of the HICSS*. Hawaii, USA

Goodhue, D. L., Lewis, W., & Thompson, R. (2012). Does PLS have advantages for small sample size or non-normal data? *MIS Quarterly, 36*(3), 981–1001.

Göritz, A. (2007). Using Online Panels in Psychological Research. In A. Joinsen, K. McKenna, T. Postmes, & U.-D. Reips (Eds.), *Oxford handbook of internet psychology* (pp. 473–485). Oxford (England): Oxford University Press.

Greengard, S. (2010). Cloud computing and developing nations. *Communications of the ACM, 53* (5), 18–20.

Gregor, S. (2006). The nature of theory in information systems. *MIS Quarterly,30*(3), 611–642.

Gronevetter, M. (1985). Economic action and social structure: the problem of embeddedness. *American Journal of Sociology, 91*(3), 481–510.

Groves, R. M., Fowler, F. J., Couper, M. P., Lepkowski, J. M., Singer, E., & Tourangeau, R. (2009). *Survey methodology*. Hoboken, USA: John Wiley & Sons.

Groves, R. M., & Lyberg, L. (2010). Total survey error: Past, present, and future. *Public Opinion Quarterly, 74*(5), 849–879.

Hair, J. F., Hult, G. T., Ringle, C. M., & Sarstedt, C. M. (2014). *A primer on partial least squares structural equation modeling (PLS-SEM)*. Thousand Oaks, CA, USA: SAGE Publications.

Hair, J. F., Ringle, C. M., & Sarstedt, M. (2011). PLS-SEM: Indeed a silver bullet. *The Journal of Marketing Theory and Practice, 19*(2), 139–152.

Harris, J., Ives, B., & Junglas, I. (2012). IT consumerization: When gadgets turn into enterprise IT tools. *MIS Quarterly Executive, 11*(3), 99–112.

Hennig-Thurau, T., Gwinner, K. P., & Gremler, D. D. (2002). Understanding relationship marketing outcomes an integration of relational benefits and relationship quality. *Journal of Service Research, 4*(3), 230–247.

Henseler, J., Ringle, C. M., & Sarstedt, M. (2012). Using partial least square path modeling in advertising research: Basis concepts and recent issues. In S. Okazaki (Ed.), *Handbook of research on international advertising* (pp. 252–278). Cheshire, UK: Edward Elgar Publishing.

Henseler, J., Ringle, C. M., & Sinkovics, R. (2009). The use of partial least squares path modeling in international marketing. In S. Zou (Ed.), *Advances in international marketing* (pp. 277–319). Bingley, England: Emerald Group Publishing Limited.

Hevner, A., March, S., Park, J., & Ram, S. (2004). Design science in information systems research. *MIS Quarterly, 28*(1), 75–105.

Hirschheim, R., & Klein, H. K. (2012). A glorious and not-so-short history of the information systems field. *Journal of the Association for Information Systems, 13*(4), 188–235.

Hoffman, D. L., Novak, T. P., & Peralta, M. (1999). Building consumer trust online. *Communications of the ACM, 42*(4), 80–85.

Huang, K.-W., & Wang, M. (2009). Firm-level productivity analysis for software as a service companies. In *ICIS 2009 proceedings*. http://aisel.aisnet.org/icis2009/21/

Huntgeburth, J., Förderer, J., Ebertin, C., & Veit, D. (2013a). How cloud computing impacts stock market prices. In *Wirtschaftsinformatik 2013 proceedings*. Leipzig:Germany.

Huntgeburth, J., Förderer, J., & Veit, D. (2013b). Up in the cloud: Understanding the chasm between expectations and reality (Research in Progress). In *Proceedings of the 34th international conference on information systems*. Milan: Italy.

Huntgeburth, J., Steininger, D., Trenz, M., & Veit, D. (2012). *Cloud computing innovation: Schritte in Richtung einer Forschungsagenda, In MKWI 2012 proceedings*. Germany: Braunschweig.

IBM (2010). *IBM acquires cast iron systems*. Retrieved 16. March, 2014, from http://www-01.ibm.com/software/websphere/announcement050310.html.

Iyer, B., & Henderson, J. C. (2010). Preparing for the future: Understanding the seven capabilities of cloud computing. *MIS Quarterly Executive, 9*(2), 117–131.

Jarvis, C. B., MacKenzie, S. B., & Podsakoff, P. M. (2003). A critical review of construct indicators and measurement model misspecification in marketing and consumer research. *Journal of Consumer Research, 30*(2), 199–218.

Jensen, M. C., & Meckling, W. H. (1976). Theory of the firm: Managerial behavior, agency costs and ownership structure. *Journal of Financial Economics, 3*(4), 305–360.

Jeyaraj, A., Rottman, J. W., & Lacity, M. C. (2006). A review of the predictors, linkages, and biases in it innovation adoption research. *Journal of Information Technology, 21*(1), 1–23.

Jiang, Z., & Benbasat, I. (2004). Virtual product experience: Effects of visual and functional control of products on perceived diagnosticity and flow in electronic shopping. *Journal of Management Information Systems, 21*(3), 111–147.

Jiang, Z., & Benbasat, I. (2007). The effects of presentation formats and task complexity on online consumers' product understanding. *MIS Quarterly, 31*(3), 475–500.

Jones, M. A., Reynolds, K. E., Mothersbaugh, D. L., & Beatty, S. E. (2007). The positive and negative effects of switching costs on relational outcomes. *Journal of Service Research, 9*(4), 335–355.

Keil, M., Mann, J., & Rai, A. (2000). Why software projects escalate: an empirical analysis and test of four theoretical models. *MIS Quarterly, 24*(4), 631–664.

Keil, M., Tan, B. C. Y., Wei, K.-K., Saarinen, T., Tuunainen, V., & Wassenaar, A. (2000). A cross-cultural study on escalation of commitment behavior in software projects. *MIS Quarterly, 24*(2), 299–325.

Kelman, H. C. (1961). Processes of opinion change. *Public Opinion Quarterly, 25*(1), 57–78.

Kempf, D. S., & Smith, R. E. (1998). Consumer processing of product trial and the influence of prior advertising: A structural modelling approach. *Journal of Marketing Research, 35*(3), 325–338.

Kim, D. J. (2008). Self-perception-based versus transference-based trust determinants in computer-mediated transactions: A cross-cultural comparison study. *Journal of Management Information Systems, 24*(4), 13–45.

Kim, D. J., Steinfield, C., & Lai, Y.-J. (2008). Revisiting the role of web assurance seals in business-to-consumer electronic commerce. *Decision Support Systems, 44*(4), 1000–1015.

Kim, K., Altmann, J., & Lee, W.-R. (2013). Patterns of innovation in saas networks: Trend analysis of node centralities. *Proceedings of the ECIS*. Utrecht, Netherlands.

Kim, S. S., & Son, J.-Y. (2009). Out of dedication of constraint? a dual model of post-adoption phenomena and its empirical test in the context of online services. *MIS Quarterly, 33*(1), 49–70.

Koehler, P., Anandasivam, A., & Dan, M. A. (2010a). Cloud services from a consumer perspective. *Proceedings of the AMCIS*. Lima, Peru

Koehler, P., Anandasivam, A., & Weinhardt, C. (2010b). Customer heterogeneity and tariff biases in cloud computing. *Proceedings of the ICIS*. Saint Louis, USA.

KPMG (2010). *From hype to future*. Retrieved 20. January, 2014, from http://www.kpmg.com/ES/es/ActualidadyNovedades/ArticulosyPublicaciones/Documents/2010-Cloud-Computing-Survey.pdf.

Krosnick, J. A. (1991). Response strategies for coping with the cognitive demands of attitude measures in surveys. *Applied Cognitive Psychology, 5*(3), 213–236.

Krosnick, J. A., Holbrook, A. L., Berent, M. K., Carson, R. T., Hanemann, W. M., & Kopp, R. J. (2002). The impact of 'no opinion' response options on data quality—Non-attitude reduction or an invitation to satisfice? *Public Opinion Quarterly, 66*(3), 371–403.

Krosnick, J. A., Narayan, S. S., & Smith, W. R. (1996). Satisficing in surveys: Initial evidence. In M. T. Braverman & J. K. Slater (Eds.) *Advances in survey research* (pp. 29–44) San Francisco, USA: Jossey-Bass.

Kuhn, T. S. (1962). *The structure of scientific revolutions*. Chicago, USA: The University of Chicago Press.

Kung, L. A., Cegielski, C., & Kung, H.-J. (2013). *Environmental pressure on software as a service adoption: An integrated perspective, In AMCIS 2013 proceedings*. Chicago: IL, USA.

Lansing, J., Schneider, S., & Sunyaev, A. (2013). Cloud service certifications: measuring consumers' preferences for assurances. *Proceedings of the ECIS*. Utrecht, Netherlands.

Lee, A. (1999). Inaugural editor's comments. *MIS Quarterly, (23:1)*, v–xi.

Lehmann, S., Draisbach, T., Buxmann, P., & Diefenbach, H. (2010). Preisgestaltung für Software-as-a-Service. In *MKWI 2010 proceedings*. http://tubiblio.ulb.tu-darmstadt.de/39293/

Lewis, W., Agarwal, R., & Sambamurthy, V. (2003). Sources of influence on beliefs about information technology use: An empirical study of knowledge workers. *MIS Quarterly, 27*(4), 657–678.

Li, Y. (2012). Theories in online information privacy research: A critical review and an integrated framework. *Decision Support Systems, 54*(1), 471–481.

Li, Y., & Chang, K. (2012). A study on user acceptance of cloud computing: A multi-theoretical perspective. *Proceedings of the AMCIS*. Seattle, Washington, USA.

Lindell, M. K., & Whitney, D. J. (2001). Accounting for common method variance in cross-sectional research designs. *Journal of Applied Psychology, 86*(1), 114–121.

Lohmöller, J.-B. (1989). *Latent variable path modeling with partial least squares*. Heidelberg, Germany: Physica.

MacKenzie, S. B. (2003). The dangers of poor construct conceptualization. *Journal of the Academy of Marketing Science, 31*(3), 226–323.

MacKenzie, S. B., Podsakoff, P. M., & Jarvis, C. B. (2005). The problem of measurement model misspecification in behavioral and organizational research and some recommended solutions. *Journal of Applied Psychology, 90*(4), 710–730.

MacKenzie, S. B., Podsakoff, P. M., & Paine, J. B. (1999). Do citizenship behaviors matter more for managers than for salespeople? *Journal of the Academy of Marketing Science, 27*(4), 396–410.

MacKenzie, S. B., Podsakoff, P. M., & Podsakoff, N. P. (2011). Construct measurement and validation procedures in mis and behavioral research: integrating new and existing techniques. *MIS Quarterly, 35*(2), 293–334.

Malhotra, N. (2008). Completion time and response order effects in web surveys. *Public Opinion Quarterly, 72*(5), 914–934.

Malhotra, N. K., Kim, S. S., & Patil, A. (2006). Common method variance in IS research. *Management Science, 52*(12), 1865–1883.

Malhotra, Y., & Galetta, D. (2005). A multidimensional commitment model of volitional systems adoption and usage behavior. *Journal of Management Information Systems, 22*(1), 117–151.

Malhotra, Y., Galletta, D. F., & Kirsch, L. J. (2008). How endogenous motivations influence user intentions: beyond the dichotomy of extrinsic and intrinsic user motivations. *Journal of Management Information Systems, 25*(1), 267–300.

Malladi, S., & Krishnan, M. S. (2012a). Cloud computing adoption and its implications for CIO strategic focus—An empirical analysis. *Proceedings of the ICIS.* Orlando, USA

Malladi, S., & Krishnan, M. S. (2012). *"Does Software-as-a-Service (SaaS) has a role in IT-enabled innovation?—An empirical analysis, In AMCIS 2012 proceedings.* Washington, USA: Seattle.

Mangold, W. G., Miller, F., & Brockway, G. R. (1999). Word-of-mouth communication in the service marketplace. *Journal of Services Marketing, 13*(1), 73–89.

March, J. G. (1978). Bounded Rationality, Ambiguity, and the engineering of choice. *The Bell Journal of Economics, 9*(2), 587–608.

Marcoulides, G., Chin, W. W., & Saunders, C. (2012). When imprecise statistical statements become problematic: A response to Goodhue, Lewis, and Thompson. *MIS Quarterly, 36*(3), 717–728.

McAfee, A. (2011). What every CEO needs to know about the cloud. *Harvard Business Review, 89*(11), 125–132.

Mell, P., & Grance, T. (2011). *The NIST definition of cloud computing.* Retrieved 19. June, 2012, from http://csrc.nist.gov/publications/nistpubs/800-145/SP800-145.pdf.

Milgrom, P., & Roberts, J. (1992). *Economics.* Organization and Management, Stanford, USA: Prentice-Hall.

Miller, L. E., & Smith, K. L. (1983). Handling nonresponse issues. *Journal of Extension, 21*(5), 45–50.

Mooi, E., & Sarstedt, M. (2011). *A concise guide to market research.* New York, USA: Springer.

Moore, G. C., & Benbasat, I. (1991). Development of an instrument to measure the perceptions of adopting an information technology innovation. *Information Systems Research, 2*(3), 192–222.

Nelson, P. (1970). Information and consumer behavior. *Journal of political economy, 78*(2), 311–329.

Nunnally, J. C. (1978). *Psychometric theory.* New York, USA: McGraw-Hill.

Nunnally, J. C., & Bernstein, I. H. (1994). *Psychometric theory* (3rd ed.). Ohio, USA: McGraw-Hill.

O'Donoghue, T., & Rabin, M. (2001). Choice and procrastination. *The Quarterly Journal of Economics, 116*(1), 121–160.

Opitz, N., Langkau, T. F., Schmidt, N. H., & Kolbe, L. M. (2012). Technology acceptance of cloud computing: Empirical evidence from german IT departments. In *HICSS 2012 proceedings.* doi:10.1109/HICSS.2012.557

Oppenheimer, D. M., Meyvis, T., & Davidenko, N. (2009). Instructional manipulation checks: Detecting satisficing to increase statistical power. *Journal of Experimental Social Psychology, 45*(4), 867–872.

Orlikowski, W. J., & Baroudi, J. J. (1991). Studying information technology in organizations: Research approaches and assumptions. *Information Systems Research, 2*(1), 1–28.

Özpolat, K., Gao, G., Jank, W., & Viswanathan, S. (2013). The value of third-party assurance seals in online retailing: An empirical investigation. *Information Systems Research, 24*(4), 1100–1111.

Parameswaran, S., Venkatesan, S., Gupta, M., Sharman, R., & Rao, H. R. (2011). Impact of cloud computing announcements on firm valuation. In *AMCIS 2011 proceedings*. http://aisel.aisnet.org/amcis2011_submissions/291/

Pavlou, P. A., & Gefen, D. (2004). Building effective online marketplaces with institution-based trust. *Information Systems Research, 15*(1), 37–59.

Pavlou, P. A., Liang, H., & Xue, Y. (2007). Understanding and mitigating uncertainty in online exchange relationships: a principal-agent perspective. *MIS Quarterly, 31*(1), 105–136.

Peace, A. G., Galetta, D. F., & Thong, J. Y. L. (2003). Software piracy in the workplace: A model and empirical test. *Journal of Management Information Systems, 20*(1), 153–177.

Penn, J. (2010). *Security and the cloud: Looking at the opportunity beyond the obstacle.* Retrieved 16. March, 2014, from http://www.forrester.com/Security+And+The+Cloud/fulltext/-/E-RES56885.

Petter, S., Straub, D., & Rai, A. (2007). Specifying formative constructs in information systems research. *MIS Quarterly, 31*(4), 623–656.

Podsakoff, P. M., MacKenzie, S. B., Lee, J. Y., & Podsakoff, N. P. (2003). Common method biases in behavioral research: a critical review of the literature and recommended remedies. *Journal of Applied Psychology, 88*(5), 879–903.

Podsakoff, P. M., MacKenzie, S. B., & Podsakoff, N. P. (2012). Sources of method bias in scoial science research and recommendations on how to control it. *Annual Review of Psychology, 63* (1), 539–569.

Pólya, G. (1945). *How to solve it: A new aspect of mathematical method.* Princeton, USA: Princeton University Press.

Popper, K. R. (1959). *The logic of scientific discovery.* London, UK: Routledge.

Popper, K. R. (1963). *Conjectures and refutations.* London, UK: Routledge and Keagan Paul.

Preacher, K. J., & Hayes, A. F. (2004). SPSS and SAS procedures for estimating indirect effects in simple mediation models. *Behavior Research Methods, Instruments, and Computers, 36*(4), 717–731.

PWC (2013). *Cloud computing—evolution in the cloud.* Retrieved 20. January, 2014, from http://www.pwc.de/de_DE/de/prozessoptimierung/assets/Cloud_computing_2013.pdf.

Ramireddy, S., Chakraborthy, R., Raghu, T. S., & Rao, H. R. (2010). Privacy and security practices in the arena of cloud computing—A research in progress. In *AMCIS 2010 proceedings*. http://aisel.aisnet.org/amcis2010/574/

Rao, A. R., & Monroe, K. B. (1989). The effect of price, brand name, and store name on buyers perceptions of product quality: An integrative review. *Journal of Marketing Research, 26*(3), 351–357.

Retana, G. F., Forman, C., Narasimhan, S., Florin, M., & Niculescu, D. J. W. (2012). *Technical support and it capacity demand: Evidence from the cloud, In ICIS 2012 proceedings.* USA: Orlando.

Richins, M. L. (1983). Negative word-of-mouth by dissatisfied consumers: A pilot study. *Journal of Marketing, 47*(1), 68–78.

Ringle, C. M., Sarstedt, M., & Straub, D. (2012). A critical look at the use of PLS-SEM in MIS quarterly. *MIS Quarterly, (36:1)*, iii–xiv.

Rogers, E. M. (2003). *Diffusion of innovations* (5th ed.). New York, USA: Free Press.

Rossbach, C., & Welz, B. (2011). *Survival of the fittest—How Europe can assume a leading role in the cloud.* Retrieved 19. June, 2012, from http://www.rolandberger.com/media/pdf/Roland_Berger_Cloud_Ecosystem_D_20111130.pdf.

Salesforce (2011). *Salesforce.com signs definitive agreement to acquire model metrics.* Retrieved 16. March, 2014, from http://www.salesforce.com/company/news-press/press-releases/2011/11/111114.jsp.

Salisbury, W. D., Pearson, R. A., Pearson, A. W., & Miller, D. W. (2001). Perceived security and World Wide Web purchase intention. *Industrial Management and Data Systems, 101*(4), 165–177.

SAP (2011). *SAP acquires success factors.* Retrieved 16. March, 2014, from http://global.sap.com/corporate-en/investors/successfactors/index.epx.

Sarker, S., Chatterjee, S., & Xiao, X. (2013). *How 'Sociotechnical' is our IS research? An assessment and possible ways forward, In ICIS 2013 proceedings.* Italy: Milan.

Sartori, G. (1984). Guidelines for Concept Analysis. In G. Sartori (Ed.), *Social science concepts: A systematic analysis* (pp. 15–85). Beverly Hills, CA, USA: SAGE Publications.

Saya, S., Pee, L. G., & Kankanhalli, A. (2010). The Impact of institutional influences on perceived technological characteristics and real options in cloud computing adoption. In *ICIS 2010 proceedings.* St. Louis: USA.

Schmitz, J., & Fulk, J. (1991). Organizational colleagues, media richness, and electronic mail—A test of the social influence model of technology use. *Communication Research, 18*(4), 487–523.

Sen, A. K. (1977). Rational fools: A critique of the behavioral foundations of economic theory. *Philosophy and Public Affairs, 6*(4), 317–344.

Shapiro, C., & Varian, H. R. (1999). *Information rules: a strategic guide to the network economy.* Boston, USA: Harvard Business Press.

Sharma, R., Yetton, P., & Crawford, J. (2009). Estimating the effect of common method variance: The method-method pair technique with an illustration from TAM research. *MIS Quarterly, 33*(3), 473–490.

Simon, H. A. (1955). A behavioral model of rational choice. *The Quarterly Journal of Economics, 69*(1), 99–118.

Singh, J., & Sirdeshmukh, D. (2000). Agency and trust mechanisms in consumer satisfaction and loyalty judgments. *Journal of the Academy of Marketing Science, 28*(1), 150–167.

Smith, H. J., Dinev, T., & Xu, H. (2011). Information privacy research: An interdisciplinary review. *MIS Quarterly, 35*(4), 989–1015.

Spence, M. (1973). Job market signaling. *The Quarterly Journal of Economics, 87*(3), 355–374.

Steininger, D. M., Huntgeburth, J. C., & Veit, D. J. (2011). A systemizing research framework for Web 2.0. In *ECIS 2011 proceedings* (pp. 1–13) Helsinki: Finland.

Straub, D. (2009). Editor's comments: Why top journals accept your paper. *MIS Quarterly, (33:3),* iii–x.

Sturgis, P., Roberts, C., & Smith, P. (2012). Middle alternatives revisited: How the neither/nor response acts as a way of saying 'i don't know'? *Sociological Methods and Research, 10*(10), 1–24.

Sun, J., & Wang, P. (2012). Community ecology for innovation concept: The case of cloud computing. *Proceedings of the ICIS.* Orlando, USA

Susarla, A., Barua, A., & Whinston, A. B. (2003). Understanding the service component of application service provision: An empirical analysis of satisfaction with ASP services. *MIS Quarterly, 27*(1), 91–123.

Susarla, A., Barua, A., & Whinston, A. B. (2009). A transaction cost perspective of the 'software as a service' business model. *Journal of Management Information Systems, 26*(2), 205–240.

Susarla, A., Barua, A., & Whinston, A. B. (2010). Multitask agency, modular architecture, and task disaggregation in SaaS. *Journal of Management Information Systems, 26*(4), 87–118.

The Guardian (2013). *How the Snowden leak is changing the tech landscape.* Retrieved 20. January, 2014, from http://www.theguardian.com/world/2013/dec/02/snowden-leak-tech-privacy-nsa-gchq-surveillance.

Thompson, R., Higgins, C. A., & Howell, J. M. (1991). Personal computing: Toward Ac conceptual model of utilizations. *MIS Quarterly, 15*(1), 125–143.

Travlos, D. (2011). *Economics of the Cloud—Can it make money?* In *Forbes* Retrieved 27. June, 2012, from http://www.forbes.com/sites/darcytravlos/2011/11/22/economics-of-the-cloud-can-it-make-money/.

Trenz, M., Huntgeburth, J., & Veit, D. (2013). The role of uncertainty in cloud computing continuance: Antecedents, mitigators, and consequences. *Proceedings of the ECIS*. Utrecht, Netherlands.

Trist, H., & Murray, H. (1993). *The social engagement of social science: A Tavistock anthology, The socio-technical perspective* (Vol. II). Philadelphia, USA: University of Pennsylvania Press.

Venkatesh, V., & Morris, M. G. (2000). Why don't men ever stop to ask for directions? Gender, social influence, and their role in technology acceptance and usage behavior. *MIS Quarterly, 24* (1), 115–139.

Venkatesh, V., Morris, M. G., Davis, G. B., & Davis, F. D. (2003). User acceptance of information technology: Toward a unified view. *MIS Quarterly, 27*(3), 425–478.

Venters, W., & Whitley, E. A. (2012). A critical review of cloud computing: Researching desires and realities. *Journal of Information Technology, 27*(3), 179–197.

Walterbusch, M., Martens, B., & Teuteberg, F. (2013). Exploring trust in cloud computing: A multi-method approach. *Proceedings of the ECIS*. Utrecht, Netherlands.

Walther, S., Sarker, S., Sedera, D., & Eymann, T. (2013a). Exploring subscription renewal intention of operational cloud enterprise systems—A socio-technical approach. *Proceedings of the ECIS*. Utrecht, Netherlands.

Walther, S., Sarker, S., Sedera, D., Otto, B., & Wunderlich, P. (2013b). Exploring subscription renewal intention of operational cloud enterprise systems—A stakeholder perspective. *Proceedings of the AMCIS*. Chicago, IL, USA.

Walther, S., Sedera, D., Sarker, S., & Eymann, T. (2013). *Evaluating operational cloud enterprise system success: An organizational perspective, In ECIS 2013 proceedings*. Netherlands: Utrecht.

Wang, Y., Meister, D. B., & Gray, P. H. (2013). Social Influence and knowledge management systems use: Evidence from panel data. *MIS Quarterly, 37*(1), 299–313.

Werts, C. E., Linn, R. L., & Jöreskog, K. G. (1974). Intraclassreliabilityestimates: Testing structural assumptions. *Educational and Psychological Measurement, 34*(1), 25–33.

Whetten, D. A. (1989). What constitutes a theoretical contribution? *The Academy of Management Review, 14*(4), 490–495.

Winkler, T., & Benlian, A. (2012). The dual role of IS specificity in governing software as a service. Proceedings of the ICIS. Orlando, USA.

Winkler, T., Goebel, C., Benlian, A., Bidault, F., & Günther, O. (2011). The impact of software as a service on IS authority—A contingency perspective. In *Proceedings of the 32nd international conference on information systems*. Shanghai:China.

Wiseman, R. M., Cuevas-Rodríguez, G., & Gomez-Mejia, L. R. (2012). Towards a social theory of agency. *Journal of Management Studies, 49*(1), 202–222.

Youseff, L., Butrico, M., & Da Silva, D. (2008). *Toward a unified ontology of cloud computing, In Grid computing environments workshop, 2008*. USA: Austin.

Zhang, Q., Cheng, L., & Boutaba, R. (2010). Cloud computing: state-of-the-art and research challenges. *Journal of Internet Services and Applications, 1*(1), 7–18.

Zhao, X., Lynch, J. G., & Chen, Q. (2010). Reconsidering baron and kenny: Myths and truths about mediation analysis. *Journal of Consumer Research, 37*(2), 197–206.

Zhu, K., Dong, S., Xu, S. X., & Kraemer, K. L. (2006). Innovation diffusion in global contexts: Determinants of post-adoption digital transformation of European companies. *European Journal of Information Systems, 15*(6), 601–616.

Zhu, K., Kraemer, K. L., Gurbaxani, V., & Xu, S. X. (2006). Migration to open-standard interorganizational systems: network effects, switching costs, and path dependency. *MIS Quarterly, 30*(1), 515–539.